Listening in Dreams

Listening in Dreams

◆

A Compendium of Sound Dreams, Meditations And Rituals for Deep Dreamers

PLUS

This is a Dream! A Handbook for Deep Dreamers

Ione

iUniverse, Inc.
New York Lincoln Shanghai

Listening in Dreams
A Compendium of Sound Dreams, Meditations And Rituals for Deep Dreamers

Copyright © 2005 by Carole Ione Lewis

iUniverse books may be ordered through booksellers or by contacting:

iUniverse
2021 Pine Lake Road, Suite 100
Lincoln, NE 68512
www.iuniverse.com
1-800-Authors (1-800-288-4677)

This is a Dream© 2000,2001
First Edition Published in 2000
By Ministry of Maat Press
Cover Art: by Nico Bovoso

ISBN: 0-595-33448-2 (pbk)
ISBN: 0-595-78326-0 (cloth)

Printed in the United States of America

Contents

Introduction

Is there a tonal order in dreams, as there is in music and poetry? I suspect there is. In these two books this order is explored and in "Listening in Dreams," the presence of sound in dreams is investigated and described specifically. This concept opens new avenues of adventure for the reader. Ione holds dreams with curiosity and love and hears their resonance, the song embedded in the dream image, the language, archetypal and personal, that emerges through dreaming. Dreams: enduring and evanescent, elusive and bold, with landscapes that are pedestrian and revelatory, sometimes simultaneously. All of these paradoxes are included in "This is a Dream!" and "Listening in Dreams."

The books describe the experience of dreaming and the skills and intuition that support using dreams as potent resources. Simultaneous meanings and a multiplicity of approaches are offered as means to cultivate dreams. Ione regards dreams and the wisdom that nourishes them with an intense focus, yet does not crush them with the weight of academic interpretation. Each dreamer's personal concept is cherished. The dreamer is understood in a variety of ways: as an individual and also, potentially, as a member of a community, one who touches the pulse of the group and presides over its well-being on many levels, including the physical, emotional, creative and spiritual.

When Ione called me and asked if I would write an introduction to "This is a Dream!" and "Listening in Dreams," I immediately remembered the way we met. As the Aboriginals say, we dreamed each other up and connected in the physical world in 1979, introduced by composer Philip Corner. To me, the meeting was more like remembering; Ione felt so familiar, our connection not so much begun as one continued. In addition to introducing the books, I want to introduce my experience of her.

Like dreams themselves, Ione is multi-faceted, many layered. She has always struck me as a woman gifted with a regard for life that perceives all of it as precious and worthy. And fascinating. Thus she imparts the artist's sense of the mythic, a sense she expresses through her way of listening. In this way, the speaker is enfolded in her high regard for their life, for their story and their dreaming. These two books are filled with that mythic quality of consciousness and they portray both dignity and humor in the approaches she suggests toward dreaming. Personable and charismatic, Ione's soft voice has great power and impact; I cannot remember ever hearing her raise her voice, yet even in large groups, people immediately focus their attention on her as soon as she addresses them and they remain engaged. In a similar way, the books are engaging, involving the reader in a rich process that encourages participation without ever shouting or admonishing. Her work is always innovative. Ione's clear intention is to share her wisdom, her lineage if you will, in spacious manner that allows for each person's individuality to emerge and flourish.

Ione has a magical presence and she carries magic in more ways than one. Many years ago, in a healing circle that I led, we were working with manifestation and using objects and pictures which we had each collected that had personal symbolic significance. Ione had been absent when I suggested that we bring these things to the circle, but on the night we shared them, she said, as each person presented what they had gathered, "Oh, I have that with me. I have that, too." And she removed from her capacious handbag pictures, crystals, drawings, ribbons. She just happened to have them all on her person, on a seemingly permanent basis. She was never without her magic, in that physical way as well as the metaphysical ways.

"This is a Dream," and "Listening in Dreams," remind us that dreams are available to all: universal nectar. All humans dream; probably all creatures as well. Ione cites research confirming how many animals dream and that babies dream in the womb. I am certain that the planets dream. Dreams, she reminds us, open the door through which the soul beckons and we cross this threshold nightly and in daylight in the shifting glimpses of waking dreams that appear in the interstices of ordinary waking consciousness.

"Listening in Dreams" cites a number of sources that focus on sound in dreams, but I found much of the material new to me, as I think it will be to many readers. In general, we are not taught a great deal about the importance of dreams and even less about the nature of sound and its intimate relationship to the meaning of dreams. Sound seems to partake of the timelessness of all dreams; it floats beyond barriers and may be perceived directly and distinctly as sound, or make itself known telepathically to the dreamer. This book describes processes that open dream experience and interpretation to include sound, to invite it and experiment with it. "Listening in Dreams" describes music in dreams and how the dreamweaver plucks a song and sings it to us in dreamtime. The dreams that are included are full of sounds, everything from sacred songs to giggles. There is a wealth of dreams, generously shared by the dreamers.

Like the author, these books are both magical and practical, with clear instructions offered in an appealing way. The suggestions are fluid, lucid and accessible, encouraging the reader to pursue dreaming with a joyful spirit, understanding that some dreams are remembered forever and others lost before morning coffee, though Ione stresses that even a tiny dream fragment is valuable. Even those fragments, she says, behave like holograms, each containing the entire world of the dream within it. Both books include a history of dream interpretation from many cultures; some techniques mirror each other, some are unique and together they offer a wide array of possibilities.

In dreams, it is said that the soul remembers what it already knows. "This is a Dream" and "Listening in Dreams" help to open the gates of memory and provoke discovery. They are a gift from the dreamers and from Ione, the author, who is a troubadour of dreams.

The Reverend Julie Rosa Winter

Listening In Dreams

I am waking up, moving through deep layers of sleep—my dream changes—a lively band is playing over in the corner of the room—a small dance floor. I step out from the table and begin to move in time to the music. I'm aware of shadowy figures watching me.

A man with a compelling deep voice moves to the microphone. Oddly, he begins to recount the daily news as I am completing my dance moves. I want to keep dancing.

But something is pulling at my attention from another place, another reality. It is…It is…Yes! I know what it is. It is my clock radio going off in another world, a world I have not yet identified as mine. The tables, the shadowy observers, the dance music, the announcer—all of these are a part of the reality of my dream world.

This sonic event is occurring during the period of time in which we rise from sleep—known technically as the hypnopompic state. Similar sound bridging can occur as we enter sleep, in the hypnogogic state—as it did for me yesterday when I found myself slumbering on the sofa. I was making a perfectly round sound—a long sound that I was attempting to direct some 100 hundred feet away so that it entered a kind of bulls eye opening with precise accuracy. I made the sound and could see it traveling toward the bull's eye. As it reached the opening, I realized I was dreaming and opened my eyes.

Simultaneously, I realize now, I was opening my *ears*. I was listening to the high hum of the fan in the corner of the room, it was making the exact pitch, the exact sound I'd been making in my dream state.

Some Definitions:

The Hypnogogic State is the cushiony time just before we go to sleep: everything becomes somewhat pliable. We are often able to influence the deeper dream state from our waking world. Many people like to play with the images and events that occur in this period, and some are able to achieve going into sleep consciously and enter into lucid dreaming in this manner. (In Lucid Dreams we know we are dreaming and stay "awake" during the dream).

The Hypnopompic State is the time just before we fully wake up. Our mind is awake but our body isn't. That 'just another five minutes before I get up' feeling is Hypnopompic. Each of these states can be termed **Hypnoidal**. that is, a state that is outside of normal conscious awareness. Other examples are what we also call "daydreaming" and "reverie" and "highway hypnosis."

◆   ◆   ◆

People are often surprised when I inquire about their relationship to sound in their dreams. The concept of sound, in this realm as in many others, such as the cinema and the theater, is more taken for granted than the visual. For instance, people may be talking to us in our dreams, and though we pay attention to what it is they are saying, we often overlook the fact that in some way we are listening to them.

But just how do we *hear* the sound of the words and other elements that come in dreams?

Does the eardrum respond to Dream Sounds, much as the eyes respond to visual dream stimuli? In 1976, Composer and dream specialist R.I.P. Hayman was a self-described "guinea pig" in the studies of sound perception in sleep done at New York's Montefiore Medical Center. These studies monitored the phenomenon called MEMA(Middle Ear Muscle Activity), assessing the feedback response of the nerve endings on the tympanic tensor muscles of the eardrum. These nerve-endings control muscle tension in response to outside sounds. During dreams these muscles twitch in response to dreamed sounds, much as eyes move tracing the movement in our perceived dream events.

Hayman describes the experience in his paper *Listening to Dreams: A project for Middle Ear Muscle Activity Audio Level Telemetry*. Using a system in which a pressure—strain gauge was embedded in a custom plastic ear mold fitted next to the tympanic membrane, the movement of the muscles was registered on a polygram, alongside REM and brain–wave readings from Electrodes. The MEMA was registered at sub audio frequencies, which none—the-less exhibited surprisingly dynamic variations. The subjectively estimated sounds were loud-85 decibels and over.

Hayman subsequently performed a preliminary experiment. The goal was to make an audio–level recording of MEMA; and during six hours of sleep in an audio studio, an attempt was made to record sounds emanating from the eardrum. Though many sounds were recorded, the results were blurred by the interference of the sounds of breathing and circulatory systems. It was apparent that in order to get an accurate result, direct access to the nerve endings would be required, which with our current technology, would be an invasive and dangerous process. Hayman speculates that eventually technology will advance enough to create a method of listening to dreams that is safe for the dreamer.

"A great new frontier could be opened, giving a wondrous wealth of imagination to the waking world," he surmises.

The Quantum Effect

Physicist David Bohm, noted for his holographic theories of the universe, believes that the world of matter, energy and mind exists as a single unbroken whole, like a hologram.

Hologram: A three-dimensional image reproduced from a pattern of interference produced by a split coherent beam of radiation (as a laser); also: the pattern of interference itself. Mirriam Websters Dictionary

Argentinian physiologist Hugo Zuccarelli has developed a sound system that he calls Holophonic. He postulates that the ear mimics the way light works to create a holographic image. This would mean that the ear creates its own reference sound and that it is able to determine the location of a sound by the resulting interference pattern that is created in the ear. Research continues on this theory.

Composer Pauline Oliveros coined the terminology *Quantum Listening* in her paper *Quantum Listening: From Practice to Theory (To Practice Practice)* presented as the Plenum Address at the International Congress on Culture and Humanity in the New Millennium: The Future of Human Values—Chinese University, Hong Kong, January 2000.

She further describes what she calls *The Listening Effect* in her book, *Deep Listening: A Composer's Sound Practice*, forthcoming from Deep Listening Publications in 2005. She writes: "As you listen, the particles of sound decide to be heard. Listening affects what is sounding. The relationship is symbiotic. As you listen, the environment is enlivened. This is the listening effect."

Hearing without Sound?

Some dream speaking/sounding is clearly aural while other such phenomena is less so. For example, there are the words or phrases that come that are simply *understood* with little or no overt sonic content. One is aware of the words and the meanings during the dream or upon awakening, without necessarily being cognizant of the *sounds* of these words.

For example, I know my grandmother was communicating with me in my last night's dreaming. But now that I think about it, I realize it was coming on what might be called a telepathic level rather than with audible words.

In a paper written for Pauline Oliveros' Deep Listening class at Rensselaer Polytechnic Institute, Theodore Zimmer writes:

"The most common sound heard in dreams, according to the people I questioned, is speech. It is usually the case where either the dreamer witnesses two or more dream characters conversing, or a dream character speaks to the dreamer, rather than vice versa. Personally, the main characters that appear in my dreams are usually people that I know: friends, family, fellow students, etc. It is not uncommon for there to be extras, such as people eating and drinking in restaurants, or people on the street. My dreams are very dialogue intensive, and I am an active participant in these exchanges. I have recently come to realize that many times the dialogue is not spoken, but understood. In other words, communication is purely telepathic, though it still holds the same principles as spoken word. For instance, telepathy, in theory, should have no boundaries: I should be able to send a message across town and still have the recipient receive it. While in spoken communication, there is a very limited distance in which sound can travel. Therefore, if I am inside my home and my communication partner is outside, he may not be able to hear what I am saying. Speaking telepathically is exactly like this: I can understand someone if they are in reasonable distance, however once they are out of range I can no longer hear them."

Listening to Grandparents and Teachers:

Some dream sounds are quite specific and don't feel telepathic at all. We seem to hear a real and recognizable voice, such as a parent or partner's voice calling our name. A friend from the Bay Area told me about her grandmother speaking to her at length about a week after her death, and this friend is clear that she was hearing the actual sound of her grandmother's voice. (Grandparents seem to have a talent for meaningful dream appearances. I plan further

research on sound characteristics as well as the timing of appearances of the departed in dreams.) It is interesting to note that this
particular visitation took place about a week after the grandmother's
death, toward morning-close to, or in the hypnopompic state in
which many have reported having visitation dreams from those who
have died.

The Hypnopompic State is also the time during which many speak
of hearing the sound of multiple voices. In my book, *This is a
Dream!* I have labeled this phenomenon "The Teachers of the
World" because the voices do sound as if they are imparting some
kind of knowledge. These "teachers" tend to come through in a
monotone–an impartial robotic or computer generated voice. The
sensation for the dreamer is as if overhearing instructions being
given to the world from what feels like an "outside" omnipotent
source.

Reading and Listening:

There seems to be a kinship between some dream sound phenomena and the sounds that move through our consciousness when we
are reading words, or reading music.

In *Listening to Reading*, (Suny Press) Stephen Ratcliffe writes:

*"The sound of words is a memory (echo) of their physical shape-space of
letters printed or drawn, of spaces between them; shape itself a memory
(echo) of their sound."*

And later: *"Readers of the visual text, as well as listeners to the acoustic one, generally pay attention to the "message" (what the writer means to say) as if the sound and shape of the words themselves don't matter or count—which of course they do."*

Some sounds in dreams seem "self arising"—coming from no particular place or person. We may ask ourselves, are any of these sounds "real"? And a small voice may wonder, "What is *real* anyway?"

In one form of Listening Meditation taught by Pauline Oliveros in her Deep Listening Retreats, she suggests that arising thoughts be treated as sound. Inter-relating with external sounds—the totality comprises a palpable sonic web.

As the meditator comes to question just how she is hearing the thoughts that arise in her mind, and as she may wonder, just who is this I, this self to whom I am so attached, so the dreamer might enquire similarly.

Certainly, when we enter the realm of dreams, we begin to expand our understanding of Reality. We enter the multidimensional world of "the dream of reality and the reality of the dream". Embracing a quantum physics perspective, we widen our understanding to include what psychologist Arnold Mindell terms *non-consensus reality* in his groundbreaking book *Quantum Mind, The Edge Between Physics and Psychology.*

Ear Worms:

Music, songs, and song fragments are common in dreams. The Germans have coined a name for pesky tunes that turn up in our sonic consciousness ; *Ahr wurm* or ear worm. Indeed, people have varied reactions to this phenomenon, ranging from bemused exasperation to real frustration.

During a discussion about ear worms at the 2004 Deep Listening Retreat at Big Indian, NY, composer Scott Smallwood shared with the group: "Usually I have some rock song in my head that is totally not what I want to be hearing at the time!"

Scott went on to tell us of a phenomenon he had just experienced that was more to his liking. During the Silent Morning portion of the retreat, the sound of the cicadas of which he has done numerous field recordings had come to him all the way from Florida, loud and clear.

Those mysterious melodies that we wake up humming are most often a part of our dream content, or are triggered by that content. Music can reference time periods in our lives with great accuracy, and so paying attention to the time frame of the music or song can assist in understanding why it is present. The same goes for the waking dream in which we all live. When a song or musical phrase "just happens" to come to our lips, it is arising from our everyday dream state and can be addressed much as any night time dream.

Sonic Puns:

We should probably never forget the great capacity of our dreams to pun. We usually take ourselves quite seriously, but our dreams like to play. Playing on words and images is a common dream phenomenon. Our dream songs' lyrics can be understood in a number of ways. For example, song snatches such as *"I think I'm going out of my mind"* or *"They call me Mellow Yellow"* or *"Who Let the Dogs Out?"* can be clear indicators of deep feeling states that are rising, harbingers of memories that are important to us at the moment…Or we might see the above examples as possible comments on feeling mindless, cowardly, and wanting to buy a pair of toe freeing sandals.

SOME SOUND DREAMS

Monique Buzzarté

Last night in my dreams I heard, listened, and played (the trombone) quite a bit in a variety of situations. Eventually in the shifting sonic dreaming scenes I dreamed that I was listening to a group's musical sounding. I was somewhere nearby, not actually in the room where this was taking place.

The exquisite beauty of this sounding grew in my consciousness into awareness, and a desire to draw closer. I followed the sounds through various hallways within the structure until I was led to the doorway where I listened some more from a few paces back, and finally inside where I listened and watched.

The doorway—a threshold and frame but no door—was set into a corner of a very large almost square room of white. There was a short row of perhaps seven, eight, or nine Deep Listening certificate holders sitting in the center of the long axis of the room, and behind them a larger number of Deep Listeners were also sitting in rows—perhaps forty or fifty people in all.

The sounding was a kind of vocal call-and-response in sense that the row of certificate holders would sound for a while, and then the larger group would answer them. The elision between the two musical forces felt like standing in that spot in the ocean where the surf pushes in while it also pulls out. The larger Deep Listener group's answer to the certificate holder's call would shift into it's own call which the certificate holders would answer, and so on, cyclically, into a time beyond time.

There was an extremely strong sense of cohesion from all those present, a solid and stable group energy that was also very dense. The interconnection and interweaving within the improvisations were fluent, and the fluidity of the sounding reflected a great mastery of intent from all present. The sounds were incredibly beautiful.

I did not recognize anyone there in this room—it seemed a different time than the one now, a time in the future. I listened and listened, listening into the sound, becoming the sound, and then later I woke. The sense of loss upon awaking—of being here now in this time instead of there then—was so great that I went back into the sleep sounding over again and again, until finally I was able to slip back into this time without feeling attached to the other. Without that attachment there was no loss; instead a feeling of empty peace.

Jukka-Pekka Kervinen
2001

I was somewhere, I do not remember where, but suddenly I begin to hear the sound of violin, very beautiful, now I notice that it was like an invitation, too.

However, the melody was the piece of Heitor Villa-Lobos: Chorus for female singer and 12 cellos *(or 8 or how many, I am not sure), but this time just the melody of alto singer, played by that violin. I start to find who is playing, I walk and walk, and suddenly I saw Devil playing that (divine) string instrument with a big smile in his face. I woke up and then I was laughing and singing very loud (that probably woke me up), I wasn't afraid, which is quite typical after seeing the most fearful demon in the universe, it just felt funny.*

That dream has been in my mind all the day. In next three minutes as I woke up, I made a little composition or exercise from that dream. It is here:

Invitation
For any number of (female) singers
By Jukka-Pekka Kervinen

All performers sit in circle. First performer turns to left and sings a sound or group of sounds, no more than three to the next performer. The listener turns to left and modifying some aspect(s) of sound(s), pitch, dynamics, order of events, sings it to the next performer. The first performer turns to right and sings another sound or group of sounds. The listener turns to right and modifying sound(s) repeat it to next performer. When performers sitting side by side both have sounds to sing, they change them again modifying some aspect(s) of sound(s), turn, and sing them to next performers. Duration of work is free. Always soft dynamics.

Caterina De Re
September 26, 2004

A Dream—Khamtrul leads me to a Sound Place:

Khamtrul Rinpoche (who is an emanation of Guru Rinpoche) and I are walking and in the distance we see a long, curving line of people leading up to a huge old stone place that looks like a church. At the end of the queue is Rinpoche's attendant, Togden Ajau (a yogi). i wonder why they are separated. But Rinpoche laughs (giggles!) and we go right to the beginning of the line at the entrance where we sit for a time under trees and shrubs. Rinpoche moves about—he makes dance movements. When he is ready we enter the space with Ajau (as he arrives), and we are greeted by the man running the space. I see that is an exhibition of ancient Chinese objects. But they are also modern too. I go over to one—it is bright blue and luminous. It looks like a long box with a slit on top and I see I can play with it with my long fingernails and it makes beautiful sounds. There are strings but it is not strung. The sound box can "sense" me. Khamtrul loves the space and moves about. I come to a huge soft sculpture, on the floor around it are big cushion—like squares. I understand them to be a 'soft keyboard'. So I play it. I realize fast as

I move down the scale and then up the scale, that whatever sound I have in my heart, I can easily manifest it outwardly as sound. It is so beautiful to do—whatever is "inside" becomes "outside"—a totally integrated sound dimension.

◆   ◆   ◆

Laura Biagi
Initiation Dream
January 6, 2003

I am at the bottom of a waterfall, with two other women. They tell me we need to climb the rocks and we start climbing, moving upwards. The stones are slippery but we are careful and we are not afraid. I can see the back of a woman climbing before me. I see her long hair. The waterfall is near us, loud, potent and benevolent. I can see the top of the waterfall; the water flows down, pulled by gravity. There is no doubt about our capacity to get there.

I reach another place that, in the dream, I know is at the top of the waterfall. I am inside a cave, inside the mountain where the water comes out, the source. There is pool of water. There are again two women. This time they are Ione and Pauline. On one side of the pool there is a place where we can walk and on the back of the pool, further away from the opening, there is a sort of a natural stone balcony. Ione and Pauline are standing there, watching…listening. I know that there is a spirit there, in this sacred place and I know that her quality is solitude. I start singing a song from Apulia, *Sola Sola* for the spirit. The text of this song talks about the wit that a woman uses to escape rape from a man who meets her alone in the street. I know this is the spirit of The Lady of the Lake. My singing is welcome.

As I sing, and because of the singing, a sacred object moves across the pool and situates itself on a sacred altar that has now appeared on one side of the pool. We proceed.

Then the two women and I want to go up in the attic of a church. I am told that in order to see what is up there, we need to go there alone, without the presence of the Catholic priest who is guarding the space. We meet the priest, who is actually a monk. He will not let us go alone and wants to come with us. We begin to run very fast up a circular staircase that has very small steps—it could be the staircase leading up a tower. The monk follows us, trying to catch us but I know we are very powerful. Our bodies are extremely potent if we can only concentrate. I wake up in the middle of the night.

Jenny Fox
Return Sound
2004

When I recall and write my dreams they most often present themselves in terms of images, actions and affect (by which I mean emotional states as they are felt in the body). My personal dream sensorium is such that it favors the visual and kinesthetic over the other senses. Yet every now and then a dream or dream state stands out for its auditory impact. Although these auditory dreams are less frequent, they are among the most striking and memorable in my body of recollected dream work.

Late one April night, back when my son was not quite a year old and I was a typically sleep-deprived new mother, I had nursed both of us into a deep sleep. Around 1:00 in the morning I was lifted into a state of semi-wakefulness by the sound of a dog walking up the stairs, its claws clicking against the bare wood of the steps and the tags on its collar jingling melodically. My first inclination was to assume that I had been dreaming, and to allow myself the luxury of drifting back into my much-coveted sleep. But as I hovered between sleep and wakefulness, I continued to hear the dog, who had by this time reached the top of the stairs and entered the bathroom, its tags continuing to jingle and its claws now clicking against the tile floor.

My husband and I have always had something of an open-door policy toward animals, and on many occasions We've allowed everything from neighbors, cats to wild birds into our house (for several years running a particular purple finch would seek refuge on extremely cold winter nights, perch on the track lighting near the woodstove, then make an assisted exit in the morning). But it had been months since our favorite visitor, a gargantuan Great Dane named Maude, had moved away, and no regular canine callers had taken her place. Our own dog, Susita, a sweet, dainty mutt with big brown eyes and bat-like ears, rescued from the Panamanian rainforest, had died about a year prior, just a month before the birth of our son. In fact the clicking claws and jingling tags I was hearing reminded me very much of Susita. The situation was worth losing some sleep over, so I roused myself into complete wakefulness and got up to investigate.

By the time I dragged myself out of bed and into the bathroom, there was no sign of the dog, and only the barely audible sound of water circulating through the heating system. I walked downstairs and looked around, but still nothing. Finally, I walked down the next flight of stairs to my husband's office, where he was seated as still and stoically as a rock before his computer, looking like he hadn't budged for hours. When I asked him about the dog he had let into the house, he simply replied, "What dog? I explained to him what had happened, and that it sounded just like Susita walking up the stairs. When Susita was alive, she would typically lie on her dog bed next to my Husband's desk into the night as he worked at the computer. At some point she would decide that it was time for a change of venue, get up, give a languorous stretch, then jingle and click her way up the two flights of stairs to the bedroom, where I was usually already sound asleep.

As soon as I mentioned Susita, my husband and I both had the same thought. I ran back up the stairs, grabbed my calendar from the year before, and looked at the date corresponding to that day, April 17. A single, terse entry read: "1:00 AM.—our Susita passed away."

Later in the day we visited Susita's gravesite in the woods behind our house, raked away the mat of dead leaves, reset the stone border, then left her an offering of water and a fresh, glistening cow bone procured from the butcher. She has since visited us a few more times in dreams, always heralded by her signature clicking claws and jingling tags. That is, until the last time my husband saw her, when she barked excitedly to get his attention, wagged her tail when he went to embrace her, then turned into a deer, as if to signal her most recent incarnation. Deer, of course, are quiet creatures by nature, but every time one wanders into my dreams now, its silence speaks of Susita.

(With special thanks to George Quasha for the title "Return Sound".)

Anne Bourne, 2004

I am playing a sound pattern on the piano as I listen to my baby inside my belly singing to me her essence, her presence. In my periphery I see composer James Tenney, gray bearded, focused, working at the piano composing from his inspiration the same sound as if in his listening he has picked up her song—and we play the patterns simultaneously.

IONE
Beyond Bearsville
Or
The Master Mechanic
1994

Dearest PO,

Thinking of you and your sandals, arriving in London. Dreamed of an area beyond Bearsville, where the road had turned to reddish clay and I, driving with an unidentified male companion, almost over-turned the car, but actually, held it in my hands, cradling it down so that we wouldn't be hurt and the car (a four wheel jeep for the rough roads) wouldn't be hurt either. I eased it down with all my strength, and we got out, before starting to look for help, I noticed that this was a very magical place. A man with long hair was wading in waist high water, right next to us, in a kind of clear pool, and pulling silver strips off the sides of it! On the other side of the road there were several people living in a contented fashion. I took a second look, because I had seen some special light coming down over their houses (all in greenery) and as I looked I saw that it was the mountain behind and that the top of the mountain overlooked them. The light was coming from there. Also there was very strong music coming from there as well, floating over the whole place, and I was interested to note that the people were living peacefully and no one seemed to mind the music, which was a popular song in instrumental version that I might have found offensive under other circumstances, but somehow here it worked and was truly lovely floating over the land. It seemed to mean that the people were happy. I think I also knew it was Sunday. I started walking back for help then, along the road, and got to a town where there were a few people, a store and maybe a post office, all very rudimentary.

I saw a sign and realized "Oh, this is Bearsville." I asked for help from someone. I needed a mechanic, a good mechanic. They said that was a problem, but then remembered that over the way I'd come from, there was someone so good that he was much in demand, and they seemed to feel it was unlikely I could swing it. Then someone else said "Oh yeah, over there they don't even have any music!"

I started to walk back the way I'd come. Back to where I'd left the car. As I arrived there, I was thinking about those others thinking there wasn't any music in this music filled place…and I was a bit fearful about the car hoping it would be alright. As I arrived I saw that there was someone (the man who'd been wading in the water I realize now) sitting comfortably sleeping with his feet propped up in the back seat. That was the end of the dream, and I realize now that he was of course the master mechanic.

◆   ◆   ◆

Anonymous
Sound Dream—From The Dream Sack
2002

As I drove along a narrow road on a high ridge, I observed a number of Cranes along the side of the road. As I was observing their beauty and magnificence, I did not see the road was partially washed out ahead. I swerved to avoid driving off the road but I was too late. When I hit the soft shoulder of red clay the Red pathfinder I was driving leaned and started to roll down the side off the cliff into a deep blue body of water far below. As I realized that the Pathfinder was sinking into the water I saw a body sinking beside the Pathfinder. I did not think this was my body because I was climbing up the cliff to the road where I could observe the car and body sinking into the deepness of the water. As I reached the road I heard very nice music and I noticed a radio in the middle of the road. I then watched another car come along and intentionally miss the radio. I then walked to the radio and picked it up and carried it to the side of the road where it was plugged into a extension cord. I noticed a phone was plugged into the same extension cord as the radio. I then noticed a boy with beautiful features sitting on the side of the road and I asked him if it was his radio and he said it was. I asked him what he wanted me to do with it and he said to just lay it where I was standing. Then a car pulled up and two women got out of the back seat of the car. I asked if the boy knew the women and he said that it was his wife. I was confused and I asked him if that was his wife because she looked too old for the boy. She looked to be in her late twenties, and the boy was too young to be married. He then denied that it was his wife. Then these two women came over and kissed the boy and proceeded into the house. I saw as the women went into the house that lines of young boys were following them. I was distracted by the display when the boy I had been talking to licked my hand and said "I like to do the monkey, go around without me." I assumed that he wanted me to go into the house. I then went to the door and opened it to the inside and saw that it was set up like a hospital with beds lining the walls. There were boys sick and dying in the beds and nurses were attending these boys. Then I woke up. The music I heard was a song with the words: "...you don't know what you got till it's gone; they paved paradise and put up a parking lot."

I felt excited and happy but a little confused about the sick and dying children in beds. I was confused about what the boy said to me. The boy licking my hand made me feel a little uneasy but mostly surprised.

The day before my dream I had been doing research for my book and was reading about sweat lodges and how Native Americans used them. I decided to go to the sauna and try to cleanse myself and have a rebirth so that I could move ahead from a painful separation from my girlfriend and get to work on my book. I meditated and tried to let go of all my past feelings of abandonment and loss.

My book relates to saving the planet by bringing the Native American ways to the attention of the modern world. Illustrating the balance between the spiritual, mental and physical parts of humanity and mother earth. I believe that our planet is sick and dying and that we need to make serious changes and feed the people of the world in order to save our selves from extinction.

My dream was in great color and detail. I have felt much better since I had the dream. Today I have felt very good and worked on my book most of the day.

I believe my book can help make a shift in the way people look at our world and humanity.

◆   ◆   ◆

A Letter From Heloise Gold
October 30, 2001

To Pauline:

I had two great dreams about you while I was in New Mexico. In the first one you were talking about what you were sure would happen when you die. You somehow were indicating that this is info for everyone; that everyone experiences this whether they are aware of it or not.

You said that at the moment of death we hear every single sound in the universe—first each one separately—one after another, then we hear one single sound that is the combo of all sounds. You said it is The Most Extraordinary Sound. As you described it I said that I understood what you were saying and that I was able to visually see the sound! The dream had a very beautiful luminous feel to it!

The next night, I dreamt that your left ear started growing right before our eyes (we were leading a Deep Listening Workshop). We knew it was growing because your hair above your ear was moving. Your ear kept getting more and more gigantic and then everyone realized that you had a Trick Ear and it was a teaching device to demonstrate Deep Listening!

◆   ◆   ◆

Pauline Oliveros
September 16, 2001

I am in a large complex trying to give a DL Workshop. I do the first part with a large group of people. Just before a break I play my French Horn. My sound is remarkably clear and excellent even though I have not played for years. I put the horn down and we take a break. I say that I will play the flute when we return.

I find the flute and begin to test it. I can play it even though I have never studied the instrument. Then I discover built in electronics on the flute. There are three different circuits. There is spoken word and harmonization. I explore the buttons and then put the flute down.

July 2004

Ione and I are leading a Deep Listening Retreat. We are walking and moving inside with the group. The energy is flowing nicely. We do a slow contact improvisation. We decide to go outside. There is water every where from the rain. The water is about 6 inches or more deep. I take off my shoes. My socks are still on. Everyone is out on the land wading. There is an embankment. My socks come off and start flowing with the current one at a time down the rock embankment. I grab one, then see the other disappearing into a hole. I grab the sock from the hole just in time. I wring out my socks. The sound of water is every where.

◆   ◆   ◆

MAKE A SPECIAL PLACE AND THEY WILL COME

Creating an ongoing dream journal or recording dreams with regularity can be very satisfying. A Dream journal will immediately assist you in every area of your life! Find the journal that is right for you—decorate it, make it outrageous. Make it yours. Change it when you want to. Try not to be obsessive about it, just enjoy it. It is a Dream Catcher. Some people use their journals for years and then grow tired of it and stop. At some point when the time is right, they often start up again.

Don't worry if you don't remember dreams every night. In fact, don't worry about anything related to dreams.

Some may want to catch dreams on a computer. Dreams adapt to computers and can thrive in cyberspace as well as in notebooks. Just make a special file for them and they will come.

Recording Dreams

When I recorded my dreams on tape during some of my early dream festivals in New York in the mid–eighties, I was impressed by the eerie quality of my voice when I played back the tapes. You could try recording your own dreaming hypnoidal voice and experience the mystery of your dreamtime self. Imagine, you could record your dream sounds on a regular basis and listen back whenever you want to.

Some Ways of Using Your Dream Journal

~ *Title*: Often titling a dream assists in pulling elements of the dream together, the way a good title will assist a poem or a short story. It can also assist if you create a lexicon for later reference.

~ *Alternate Title or Sub Title*: There may be a second title that appeals, or a sub-title that further speaks to the subject matter of the dream.

~ *Theme*: A dream may have one primary theme or several going at once that are of importance to the dreamer. Identifying ongoing themes can give you important information about the "weather" of your psyche.

~ *Feeling*: Dreams have the ability to show us what we are feeling. At times when we are more unaware of our interior workings than others, this can be extremely helpful.

~ *Sound quality*: How does sound operate in the dream? Do you hear the sounds in the same way as in waking life, or differently. What kind of sound phenomena do you notice?

~ *Aura of the dream*: A subtle feeling or visual sensation emanating from the dream. Often this lingers beyond the overt memory of the dream, or may be what is present instead of other more 'concrete' imagery.

~ *Associations*: Try: "What does this remind me of?" "When did I last feel this way?" or "This dream makes me think of…"

~ *Extrapolate*: Move from specifics to larger groupings. Instead of "In my dream Jim takes a high speed train to Amsterdam—a place I've never been," try "A man in my dream is moving super fast to a foreign (i.e., unknown) place. This may resonate with your own fast paced life in which you sometimes wonder where you're going.

~ *Mapping Features*: Make a map in your dream journal of places-landscapes, or architectural elements, room locations in a house, and so on. You may be surprised at how helpful this is in opening up your dream for you.

~ *Questions to parts of the dream*: Ask any part of the dream a question (or questions) that you have about them, such as "What are you doing in my dream?" Or "Why are you so angry with me? What would it take to make you happy?" Hang loose in a kind of dreamy state and see what answer comes. Write it down. A full dialogue may ensue which will give you lots of information.

~ *Question from the dream*:
-What question is this dream asking me?" Jot it down.
-How active or passive am I in this dream?" The answer to this will simply show you how things are going in your waking state. Chang-

ing the dynamic in waking state will shift the dreams. Changing the dynamic in your dreams will shift your waking state.

-*Play with the Dream*—paint, draw, dance and generally have fun with your dreams. Be more like your best dreams in waking state.

Trust in the Dream

Some of us are frustrated when we do not remember our dreams. Often people will say to me right off when I start talking about dreams, "I don't remember my dreams." Sometimes what they really mean is that they don't remember every night. If you are remembering a few important dreams in any given month, you are definitely "remembering your dreams." If you would like to remember every night, then you can create an atmosphere that will encourage more frequent recall (See *This is a Dream!*).

Dreams have a kind of periodicity that we can actually trace. If you are keeping a journal, you could begin to notice when you remember more dreams. Notice the cycles of the moon, the cycles of your body, the proximity of bed partners, medications, food, etc. All have an effect on our dreaming and dream recall.

Trust that you can have your dreams by creating Dream Space in your sleeping environment. For some of us, this may mean taking time out from stressful situations, going on retreats, changing the furniture in the sleeping room, removing distracting elements that are in close proximity.

I know what your dream means!

Remember, when receiving another person's dream *do your best to avoid telling them what you think it means*. Actually, even if you do tell them what you think it means for them, you will more than likely be saying more about what it means to you. Dreams have the wondrous ability to be extremely personal and at the same time, communal and non-local. An agile dream can easily take a quantum leap from one dreamer to another. As you respectfully feel your way into another's dream, it can open new meanings for you and if skill-fully shared, new meanings for the dreamer as well.

Relaxing with Dreams Good or Bad:

Nightmares or *Bad Dreams* can be eased by trying to *relax* around the content of the dream. Generally we tend to tighten around these dreams and tightening only strengthens the fear. We push away the unwanted material and we may think we're getting rid of it, but it is still *somewhere*–compartmentalized and split off and ready to become much more dangerous to our psyches. Relaxing may mean breathing deeply and not jumping to conclusions about the dream. Writing or telling the dream to a friend or a therapist can loosen the grip of the fear and even bring an understanding of the dream that is helpful rather than alarming. Seeing the dream as a source of infor-mation and a tool for healing rather than as an unwanted adversary can help enormously.

Dream Partners

A dream partner can be any friend or family member with whom you can share your dream experiences. A dream partner is a psychic support. Your partner can hold the space for your dreaming, be a sustaining and comforting element.

In the Deep Listening Workshops, Women's Mysteries Workshops, and Dream Circles that I facilitate, there is usually a time when I designate or ask participants to choose a partner. This partner is simply holding the space for dreaming on whatever topic we have going for that time. A partner can also be there for exploring the dreams in the morning and assisting in unfolding the mysteries and revelations of the night.

A *Dream Pod* is a group of three or more in a larger group who explore their dreams together.

Dreaming For A Partner

Incubating a healing dream for another person can be fascinating. It can be attempted without consciously knowing anything about the other person—just by going to sleep and stating your intention. Or the healing dream can be undertaken after talking with the person and finding out what is needed.

The resulting dreams often show up with an "overlay" of the themes and imagery of the dreamer. But once discussed, the dreams can be shown to have meaning for the receiver. Sometimes the dreams are quite direct, however and practically shout out the name of the one dreamed for.

Dreaming In a Group

Dream Groups-facilitated and non-facilitated are pleasurable and interesting ways of creating dream community. Many dream groups exist on the Internet and I have had wonderful experiences with dream sharing in this manner. You could start your own e-group or regular informal group or join a pre-existing group.

Dreams are a unifying resource. Any group of people who begin to share their dreams together becomes noticeably more homogenous within a matter of minutes. Sometimes, the homogeneity is revealed to have preexisted the formation of the group. Synchronicities occur-similar or identical themes, images and stories emerge. This phenomenon is sometimes called "Dream Weaving."

The Maori people gather together to sleep and dream in one building to induce a healing dream for an ailing tribe member. The ancient Egyptians, and later the Greeks had Dream Temples in which many people gathered, hoping to receive a healing dream. Under certain circumstances and at special temples, it was also possible to have a priest or priestess dream a healing dream for you.

The Dream Festival

I have created a month long Dream Festival in Kingston, NY for a number of years. The Festival is an area wide and international tribute to dream awareness that includes expressions of all the arts, and we usually have one overnight concert, during which the participants bring their bedding and sleep in the Gallery at Deep Listening Space together. In the morning we have breakfast and tell the dreams. R.I.P. Hayman's seminal work, *Dreamsound; Concert for Sleeping Audience* was performed three years in a row at The Gallery at Deep Listening Space. Originally composed in 1986 and performed at New Music America's Houston Festival, and later presented at *The Kitchen* in New York City as well as at other venues, *Dreamsound* is an event for sleeping audience based on the acoustic and social phenomenon of sleep. It is a musical event which encourages relaxation, comfortable sleep and pleasant dreams. During one concert, we were delighted find our dreams were being infiltrated by a beautiful Dawn Raga being played by master flautist's Steve Gorn. Steve had slipped into the nearby office in the morning to bring us this sonic treat.

Composer and Sound Specialist Seth Cluett has also performed throughout the night for dreamers at the gallery. Cluett's piece *Moraine Shoal* utilizes a number of oscillators which are tuned to the room. Additional oscillators use data acquired from glacial sites to control the pitch-change and volume-change. Cluett explains, "The performance is a disciplined action in which I control the speed of some of the changes at a very slow rate. The speed of change is determined by my muscular system's ability to perform the action."

A few comments on one morning in October 2003:

Phillip Gurrieri: "It felt like the engine room of a ship—a dream within a dream. My body oscillated like a sign wave, my arms moved like a gyroscope. The bird sounds in the morning were very clear."

Laura Biagi: "I heard the sound while I was sleeping upstairs. The sound broke down knots in my body."

Sarah Weaver: "The pulse of sound transferred to the sound of the rain and the plumbing. I went into a dream consciousness...a very dark place. I woke up with the realization that everything I need is here."

Ione: "I felt a cushiony synchronicity–similar to being in Egypt. I felt a deep sense of community."
Pauline Oliveros: "I gained a better understanding of some kind of synchronicity of cells and neurons."

Nancy Graham and her partner Henry Lowengard presented an evening of their dream related work during the 2004 Dream Festival. Nancy creates Somniloquies—dream poems on the edge of sleep.

Nancy describes her unique and fascinating work in this manner:

"I create the somniloquies by recording myself while reading aloud a written passage repeatedly at bedtime. I select a text that I respond to strongly in some way, whether because I loved it when I was younger, because I passionately agree or disagree with what it says, or because I find the language beautiful. As I grow sleepy, the reading grows more chant—like and meditative. After roughly twenty minutes of reading, I begin to deviate from the written text, yet the act of reading keeps me awake enough to return to reading. For the following twenty minutes or so I will read, sleeptalk and doze.

Somehow the process follows its own arc and when I'm 'finished,' I awaken to turn off the recorder and the light. I transcribe the recording the following day and edit it to use as the basis of poems and sound pieces.

A sampling of the results of Nancy's dream time reading of the children's classic *Good Night Moon* by Margaret Wise is as follows:

Bedtime Story

In the great green room
There was a telephone
And whatever you mean

And apologies, no dimples
That's what you say

Goodnight room
Goodnight moon
Ray's changed a lot this winter
I'm still feeling that it'll be ok
You don't have to dress up to go
I wonder who left a pot on the floor so I
could stub my toe

In the great green room
There were three things running through his head
and there were three tables of food

and there were three little bears sitting on chairs
and they thought it'd be a good place to wait inside

In the great green room
there was a television
there was a teddy bear
and teardrops? or only teddy bears?
A teddy bear or two, Japanese
looked like they were having fun, sounded like a chant

In the great green room there was a teddy bear and a phantom
In the great green room there was a teddy bear and a hot flashlight
In the great green room there was a teddy bear and a kind of relief

There were three little bears sitting on chairs
These are from past car inspections
(Need to spit up, Ada?)

Goodnight to Wendy and Catherine
We're staying here a long time
Engage the oxen

In the great green room there was a triumph for Oz
and a picture of—
There were several things there

How about the cow jumping under the moon?
That'd be good
Or a sea cow?

There was a headphone
and a picture of—
Look at all the scraps you have, Kate
She was jumping over the horizon
I don't think that was her

The patch you get in your arm
to show us where the blood stops flowing
if it were to stop flowing

In the great green room
there were the three confident ways
and a part of being tough
is also to be honest and helpful

In the great green room
There was a minute
A moment—

◆   ◆   ◆

Composer Norman Lowrey has been an integral part of many
Dream Festivals. He has lovingly created a family of numinous
Singing Masks through the years. Mask performances include audi-

ence participation in a magical community ambiance. The score for his most recent performance is as follows:

Private Prayers/Public Rituals I

by Norman Lowrey

"All finite things reveal infinitude…"—Theodore Roethke

Every location, however small or seemingly insignificant, may be thought of as a holographic image containing the whole, a kind of portal into infinity. With this in mind, all present are invited to select a small territory anywhere within the gathering space, to listen intently, and to offer a prayer to/through this portal. This localized, particular place may be thought of as an altar. Feel free to temporarily rearrange anything in this space, to add your own objects, to contribute further to making the space sacred. Your prayer may be completely silent or vocalized in any way you wish. As you pray, Singing Masks will function as resonators, amplifying all prayers into DreamTime. A soundscape of Singing Mask private prayers together with dreambird sounds will accompany the public ritual.

◆   ◆   ◆

Deep Listening Certificate Holder Raylene Campbell is a Canadian Composer and accordionist who is creating work inspired by the dreaming process.

She writes: 'I Dream Eye' is becominga big dream pun.

I Dream Eye =

Eye Dream I"

I Dream Eye is essentially an exploration, documentation, and reflection of dream as it exists in many levels and experiences of consciousness. This is an audio/video art performance piece using a modified version of the New Expanded Instrument System (EIS), (A performance system developed by Pauline Oliveros) video sculpture, accordion, and of course dream.

'I Dream Eye,' will involve the creative exploration of dream, the transitions and connections of moving from unconscious awareness into conscious awareness, and dreambody. In his book *Memories, Dreams, Reflections* C.G. Jung wrote 'The dream is the small hidden door in the deepest and most intimate sanctum of the soul, which opens into that primeval cosmic night that was soul long before there was a conscious ego and will be soul far beyond what a conscious ego could ever reach.'

My creative process for this production will be extensive and will involve the practice of keeping a daily dream journal (as I have for five years). As I experience more profound or lucid dreams I will explore the dream creatively through my awareness of the sound environment, visual environment, dreambody, (See the work of Arnold Mindell in Bibliography of these pages.) and improvisation. As I will be continuously creating performance pieces via dream exploration it is important that the memory and feeling of the dream remain clear and vivid as I create each performance piece. Not only will I be exploring the 'story' of these dreams, but also the physical waking experience of the dream. This will manifest through a practice of expanding my improvisational skills while the dream is still fresh.

My creative vision is to explore the transitions and connections of moving from dreaming life to waking life, of moving through various forms of consciousness by contemplating sleeping dreams as well as body/mind experiences of conscious/waking dreams, and to 'project' these experiences through creative performance.

Vonn New: Dreaming in the Proximity of Mars.

A series of pieces based on a community of dreams collected during the three weeks before and after Aug 27, 2003—when Mars and Earth were at their closest point in the last 60,000 years.

The dreams were collected by putting out a Call for Dreams to various email lists, including DeepListening List Serve and Loud Zoo Fans. Loud Zoo is my band. Some people submitted dreams in text form in emails. Marc Jenson, a member of DeepL, recorded a dream on cassette tape and mailed it. In addition, dreams were collected in person from members of Loud Zoo, and at Passa-Grille beach (near St Pete Beach) during a Women In Black peace event. I recorded one dream of my own, which was a waking dream that I had during a movement improvisation at the 2003 Deep Listening retreat at Big Indian, NY.

This collection of text and audio dreams formed the basis of all three pieces with elements from each informing those to come.

Version 1—Installation at the Paladium theater great room, St Petersburg, FL, EMIT series concert, 9/30/2003.

The idea was to create a tangible representation, that people could move through, see and hear, of a dream community after the dreamers have moved on. I was depicting a community of dreams, rather than a community of dreamers. In order to communicate the idea of a community, I presented the collect dreams along with an infrastructure that served to link and network between the dreams themselves.

I created 7 little beds. The little beds were really nothing but blankets, comforters and a sleeping bag folded to resemble a bed and placed on the floor with a pillow. I arranged them in 2 rows, a row of 3 and a row of 4. As I collected dreams, I allowed the character of the dreams to influence my selection of bedding. Each bed was arranged on the floor with a collection of accessories: 1 bed was a sleeping bag with a flashlight, water bottle, insect repellent, pen and journal next to it. Another bed was a moon and stars theme with a lamp, Harry Potter book, glasses and magic wand. One was all bold solids with a box of condoms and a glass of water. Another was floral print comforter with an array of vitamins, pills, lotions, and glasses (thankfully, I did not think to add a glass w/false teeth until afterwards)

The little beds were uninhabited, except that I fluffed them up and then lay down on each one to leave an impression of my body. Nestled on each pillow, in the indentation of the absent dreamer's head, was an old fashioned cassette tape recorder.

I sifted and sorted through the dreams and made 7 cassette tapes (one for each little bed) with the dream-tellings repeating in a loop.

The dream tellings on the tapes were complete tellings with out any editing. On some beds, 2 or more dreams by different people were told sequentially. Other beds were a single dream repeating.

The infrastructure for the dream community was a network of pipes, Dream Plumbing, that carried the sound of dreams from the little beds and allowed them to fragment, intermingle and interact with one another. I built a structure out of black-painted pipe that the audience walked through like a tunnel. Because of the bendiness of pipes, it wasn't particularly rigid and had a slightly disconcerting (to lawsuit-paranoid theater owners) bouncy vibration.

The Dream Plumbing system consisted of a backbone of pipe that ran down the center of the rows of beds above the heads of the audience. 7 smaller pipes ran out from this backbone, straight out for a foot and a half, then straight down for 7.5 feet then out to the little bed, where it ended right at the indention of the pillow, against the speaker on the tape player. After getting the construct assembled, it sagged in the middle and looked something like a giant, warped ant with an extra leg.

The sound from each dream-telling tape travelled through the pipe, up into the backbone where the sounds from all the dreams would get mixed up. Openings in the bottom of the backbone pipe let the dreams fall out onto anyone who choses to walk through. I'm not sure if this actually happened acoustically, but that was the intention.

The Dream Plumbing structure was painted with words and images from dream fragments in pale yellow/orange/white acrylic paint. A 22 inch frame drum painted with acrylic ink to look like a Mars was hung from the structure with a mallet hanging nearby, as was a gong w/a mallet, and several sets of windchimes.

All the dreams that were collected in text form were hand printed in black ink onto a large piece of sheer white fabric-the Dream Veil.

At the end of the tunnel, a home—made percussion instrument made from chimes was placed. Raihan Alam, a percussionist and member of Loud Zoo played the role of the Dream Listener. Both Raihan and the instrument were draped with the dream veil. Raihan was instructed to listen to the dreams and the audience and to react by playing the instrument, but to move as if he is doing Tai Chi. Raihan could only be seen by peering through the mist of the dreams (the veil). Next to Raihan was a large cushion.

The audience was instructed in how to interact with the installation by cards with pictures of Mars. They were led to walk through the structure by a pathway of the cards on the floor. The mallets and wind chimes had cards that said "Swing". The cushion next to Raihan had a card that said, "Tell your own dream here."

The lighting was kept low and dreamy.

People moved through, interacting with each little bed. Could stop and listen to a dream all the way through, could move through the center and hear different dreams coming from all directions.

Version 2—Belly Dance Ballet and Sonic Improvisation.

Performed at Viva La Frida, Tampa FL, Nov 7, 2003.

After the installation was over, the richness of the dream collection demanded a performance piece. Loud Zoo had been experimenting using story telling and themes in dance, which is not typical of belly dance.

I wrote a soundtrack which I recorded onto CD. The piece was performed live by the Loud Zoo band improvising to the accompaniment of the sound track with dance by the Loud Zoo Tribe and guest dancers Evelyn Tosi and Shirley Kathleen.

The timeless, mixed up, intermingling quality of dreams that was apparent in the installation was achieved by editing the dreams down to fragments and placing them into the soundtrack.

I listened to all the dreams sequentially, over and over, until I discerned the common themes shared across the dreams. These themes were:

1. the nature of dreams themselves

2. Longing/Desire

3. Relationship

4. Reptiles

5. Predation

6. Color

7. Healing

After finding these themes, I continued to listen to the dreams while allowing myself to move freely. I placed cards with the themes one the floor and let myself move to the card that I was feeling as the dreams were playing. I edited the dreams and placed the fragments into a lexicon that I created for each theme.

The accompanying sounds in the soundtrack were created using AudioMulch software on a PC. The primary sound is a bass drone of oscillating harmonic waves. There were two effects intended by the bass drone. 1) I read that people report 'religious experience' in cathedrals more often when the barely-audible bass notes of pipe organs are played. I wanted to use very low pitches to deepen the dream experience. 2) The left and right stereo channels are of different frequencies and oscillate at different rates—this to resemble the bilateral stimulus of EMDR therapy. In addition, small percussion and other acoustic sounds, such as crinkly plastic, paper clips, note cards, and a creaky mic stand were played through an Audiomulch comb filter to add texture.

Individual dancers or groups of dancer were given sections of the piece. They listened to the soundtrack and decided how to depict the theme and whether to choreograph or improvise their sections.

A three—way dynamic developed within the piece between 1) Mars, which seemed to emanate from the bass drone of the soundtrack and also from the band and the images of the planet projected onto a screen at the back of the stage 2) the dreams, depicted by the dancers and 3) the Dream Listener, this time played by dancer Johanna Krynytzky as well as the band and the audience.

When dancers were not actively dancing a part, they were 'sleeping' in a big puppy pile on the corner of the stage.

The band improvised with drums, flutes, viola, and wine glasses. Evelyn Tosi danced solo for Longing and Healing. Shirley Kathleen, a professional contortionist from Brazil, danced reptiles. The full Loud Zoo dance tribe danced Relationship and Color. A duet of Loud Zoo dancers Cate Alam and Kimberly Freed danced predation. As Dream Listener, Johanna Krynytzky danced the transitions and occassionally effected change with judicious use of the Dream Veil.

At the end of the piece, the dancers each carry a windchime through the audience and away, fading into the distance.

Version 3—Installation
Deep Listening Space, Kingston NY, Oct 2–28, Ione's Dream Festival.

This installation freely borrows elements from the first 2 versions.

The Altman room was draped in black material and painted with dream fragment words and images, reminiscent of the Dream Plumbing from v1.

The Dream Veil was hung over the window, so that light will filter into the room through a mist of dreams.

The frame drum and windchimes from the first installation are suspended from the ceiling.

The soundtrack and slides from the performance piece form the sound and visual components.

In addition, a few physical props, reflected in the dreams are scattered through the room as well as Dream Catcher scented oil.

The lighting is a dreamy red, created by strings of decorative lights run along the floor and the chair rail along the wall.

Michelle Nagai
hand holding station

hand holding station #1 (a work-in-progress)

The concept for Hand Holding Station came about while participating in one of Pauline Oliveros' Deep Listening ® Retreats. I was struck by the simple efficiency of listening as we practiced it, sitting quietly in a space with others, gathering up awareness of the room, the world outside the room and our own internal functions. An enormous number of dreams, emotions and memories revealed themselves to me during these listening sessions.

Hand Holding Station #1, a performance-installation, is fundamentally concerned with exploring the awareness of self that comes about through direct physical connection with another. In this context, "self" is understood as both a physical self (the audience members and performer, sitting together in a room) and an extended "dream state" self (the shared, disembodied mind activity of performer and audience members).

Using various custom built physiological sensors (respiration sensor, blood volume pulse sensor, galvanic skin response sensor, temperature sensor etc.) I will monitor and record my body's changing states as I lie, sit and otherwise inhabit the installation for extended periods of time. This biofeedback data will be used to algorithmically control sonic and visual events occurring within the space. Based on documented dream recollections culled from a variety of personal and public sources, these events will consist of fleeting compositions that respond to and re-interpret the dreams as abstracted moments of sound and image.

The space for the installation will be organized so that visitors may sit privately with me and make physical contact with my body, thus having a direct impact on the input to the sensors that I'm wearing. As my biofeedback responds to these individual interactions, visitor-specific environmental shifts will take place within the space as a result. By creating an intimate and singular experience for each visitor, I mean to bridge the physical and the dream state selves, and cause the audience to feel as if their own thoughts in the moment are being made manifest on the walls and in the air around them as dream-like visions and sounds.

Ongoing Dream Groups

Group dreaming requires skillful and compassionate processing and patience to allow the group message to emerge.

You could try having several members of a group divide into smaller groups to dream for one person who needs special assistance. Or you could ask the entire group to dream for a person or a situation. This is a wonderful way to keep in touch with the needs of the community.

In a weekly or monthly group, members of the group could feature one person's dream each week while giving some time to each person's dream experience. For large groups, creating partners will give each person a chance to tell a dream.

Working on the dream can consist of:

~ Having the dreamer enact the dream

~ Having several or all of the group members enact some or all of the dream while the dreamer watches

~ Members could take turns exploring the dreamer's dream from their own personal perspective

~ Creating vibrant art work related to each dream

~ Creating a group art work (on a single large sheet of paper) based on one or more dreams

Petitioning the Dreaming Self

Dream Incubation

Dream Incubation is a millennia old way of gathering information from our dreams. Dreaming on a question, a problem or a creative concept can bring rewarding solutions. Many composers, writers, painters and other artists rely upon their dreams for guidance.

The Best Method of Incubation is Being in touch with our Dreaming:

Many methods exist. But the best one to my mind, is to recognize that we are always being offered new information in our dreams, and much of this information is giving us the very answers we are seeking, whether we consciously ask this of them or not. What if we could actually trust in this?

In *Dreaming While Awake* (Hampton Roads Publishing Co.), Arnold Mindell shows that we are dreaming 24 hours a day. The seeds of our dreams are available to us at all times. We can be in the state of lucid dreaming all the time. The benefits of this are that we are able to solve our difficulties in relationships, health and work. As we become more and more attuned to our dreams, and the roots of our dreaming, we begin to understand our own symbols and stories organically. We start living closer to our essence in waking state, and so we begin to experience a new sense of well-being and ease.

A Matter of Fact Method for Night Time

You can write out a petition to your dreaming self, then boil it down to a simple question about the subject on which you are seeking guidance-fold it up, put it under your pillow, keeping a pen and journal or notebook close by, and see what comes. Give the dreamtime a few nights and something of assistance is bound to come.

Method Based On An Ancient Egyptian Incubation:

Requirements:

A small bowl of spring water

A white candle

A small metal bowl or container

A small box

In the morning or some time during the day, write out your request on two small pieces of paper. Float one paper in the bowl of water. Place the other paper beneath the bowl of water. In the evening, find a special quiet time before bed to light the white candle. Take the paper out of the water. Place it in a small box. Holding the other piece of paper, begin making a chant or other vocal rendition of your petition. Vocalize until it sounds really good to you. Allow the words to fill the room. Continuing your sounding, burn the paper carefully in the flame of the white candle. Save the ashes in a small box near your bed. Snuff out the candle. Keep the bowl of water close to the head of your bed after placing a little on your forehead.

Go into sleep softly intoning your Dream Chant. Add simple prayers to Dream Spirits or to your favorite deity at will.

Where's my Dream Answer?

If there should be a time when you have requested guidance and cannot recall the dream content of the evening, try relaxing around whatever you do recall, however vague, however subtle. Try allowing the subtle feelings and the 'aura' of the dream to be present.

Try trusting that the information you requested is with you and available. And most important, practice being gentle and compassionate with yourself. Your dreams of guidance will come to you soon. Enjoy the incubation process for three days to a week. Then take a break.

If you have requested guidance and the dreams that come do not seem to give you the answers you are seeking, try using some of the methods of playing with dreams in this book or in *This is a Dream* to assist in unfolding their messages to you. It is always good to share the dreams with another person who is familiar with your process.

It is important not to try too hard. Dreams really don't like to feel pressured. Know that your guidance resides in them none-the-less. Understand that you can "*know without knowing.*" Remember that you already have the answers. You are merely attempting to coax them a bit closer to your fully conscious state.

◆   ◆   ◆

A FEW MORE MEDITATIONS AND EXERCISES

Listening to the Dream Character

Become a character in one of your more interesting dreams. Begin to find the vocal quality of that character. Try remembering some of the words or sounds of that character or allow yourself to find these words or sounds spontaneously arising. Let your character speak in a more and more fluid manner, without thinking about what the words mean. Ask your partner to mirror back to you your character's words and sounds. Listen to what your character has to say (This exercise can be effective with a partner. If you are alone, a tape recorder, or video camera could be utilized).

Humming Into Sleep

Go into sleep softly humming to yourself. Find the pitch and key that feels most comforting and healing. Allow the humming to float through the body, softly directing it to places where there is the most tension, discomfort or pain. Allow yourself to go into sleep in this manner, following the sound of your hum. Notice the quality of sleep and dreams on nights when you have hummed.

Sounding and Moving with Energy

Jung was always interested in where the energy in his patients' dreams was heading. Consider where the energy in your dreams is going. Feel it and begin moving with it. While moving, find the sound of this energy and opening your mouth for easy egress, allow it to float from your throat and mouth.

Amplifying and Transforming

Remember an important dream. Listen to the feelings in the dream. Begin to sound and move with the feelings. Find the direction the energy is going. Establish. Then take it further.

If it is going in a direction you like, amplify it.

If it is going in a direction you'd rather not go toward, transform the elements of the dream using movement and sound.

Dream Song Fragment Exercise

Amplify the song fragment that is going round in your head. Sing it or play it on an instrument. Notice words, phrases or associations that arise. Notice feelings that arise. Treat the song as a sacred gift. Own it. Thank it, and explore for yourself what is has to offer you. Consider the song as a signal of new power and understanding for you.

Dream Sound Duet

Sound your dream to a partner, without words. Just let the sounds arise spontaneously as you recall feelings from the dream. Take turns listening and receiving the dream sounds. Then, when it feels right, begin to sound together in a Dream Sound Duet.

If you like, expand to small, then larger gestures and listening to each other, move about the room, following the feeling of your sounds while vocalizing.

The Best Dream You Ever Had

While sitting by yourself, remember the most wonderful dream you ever had. Relive the feelings of that dream. Let them spread throughout your body. When you feel ready, speak the words that want to come and make the sounds that feel right to express these good feelings. Move around if you wish.

The Best Dream They Ever Had–Flower Form (For a group)

Ask a large group of people to form a standing or sitting circle. Evoke the concept of the best dream each person has ever had. It could be a dream from long ago. Or it could be a recent dream. Whatever dream comes, it is the right one. Ask them to gently close their eyes, or to look down toward the floor. Let them establish the feeling of that dream. Suggest that they allow the feelings of the dream to spread throughout their bodies. Suggest that they isolate one particular part of the dream. This would be the most important part to them right now. Suggest that each person can let the words associated with the dream float out into the room at will, in no particular order. Listen to the floating words until they spontaneously stop.

Suggest that the group notice the feeling in the room. This is the feeling of their group dream.

Dreaming for the Ancestors

Remember a dream that you had about an ancestor (either known or unknown) who is not living. If you don't remember a dream, bring up a memory or an imaginary scenario concerning this ancestor. Allow the words and sounds this ancestor wants to make to arise. Speak them out. Move around the room being this ancestor. Listen for any words of guidance that this ancestor may have for you.

Dreaming the Sounds of the Universe

Listen in your waking and sleeping dreams for the sounds of the universe. Perhaps they can be heard in the spaces between sounds. Perhaps we are hearing these sounds all the time without knowing, without recognizing them.

"We are dreaming this!" intones Dream Mask Maker Norman Lowrey in one of his Singing Mask performances. Let us live the dream fully. Let us listen and enjoy it.

END

This is a Dream!

◆

A Hand Book For Deep Dreamers

By Ione

For my father, who is dreaming.

"—Dreamlike states of consciousness are the basic substance of the universe. Matter is created from dreaming." Arnold Mindell, Quantum Mind, Lao Tse Press

The Dream Keeper Speaks:

The dream processes in this handbook have emerged from contact with many dream worlds, my own as well as those of other dreamers. As a child, I loved having my special world of dreams for company during the night. And when I became a mother of small children, I enjoyed gathering and recording their dreams.

"Mickey Mouse told me Hi!" exclaimed my two and a half year old first born son, Alessandro one morning. It was 1972, and we were in the kitchen of our stone farm house in the South of France. We were living without electricity or telephones, there were cherry trees out front, poplars out back; and the rising sun and the setting moon appeared together in the sky many mornings. Dreams were often the subject of our drawings and paintings and conversations. It was here that I noticed that all of our dreams including those of the children's father, Salvatore, began to show what I call "interweaving". There were striking examples of similarities in our dream content. For example, on the simplest level, on any given night, each of us would have at least one dream object or characteristic in common.

Soon my other sons, Nico and Antonio began telling and writing their own dreams; and later when they were older, in other cities and countries, they were active participants in many of my dream workshops and dream events. Antonio wrote his collection of dream poems, *Cats in Black Shoes* at the age of 8. Alessandro and I are collaborating on a children's book inspired by his dreams. Nico, a visual artist has designed the cover of this book using a photograph taken by my grandson, Antonio Hylan Bovoso.

One day it became clear to me that I really wanted to make an even stronger commitment to the idea of bringing dreams and dream work into every area of my life. I was already incorporating dreams into my writing as a natural course, using them as inspiration for poetry as well as larger works of fiction and non-fiction. While researching material for my memoir, *Pride of Family; Four Generations of American Women of Color*, I relied upon my dreams to guide me through the territories of my emotions. I also received constant assistance with creative ideas.I gained access to the "timeless" realms in this manner, and felt closer to centuries past in consciousness.

I also began doing "Dream Weavings" of different kinds at parties and other gatherings of people. Essentially, "Dream Weaving" involves the evocation of dream themes, characters, objects, and feelings in a communal setting.

Many of my dream workshops and retreats were held in New York City at my Chambers Street loft, *The Center for Live Letters*. Others were held in the parlor of my upstate New York home. Others took place and continue to be offered in New Mexico, Colorado, France, Spain, Morocco, Hawaii and Egypt.

"Dreams never lie!" I like to say. This usually gets everyone's attention; and of course, it is a marvelous truth that no matter how outrageous their scenarios, or how complex their symbolism ; they never lie about feelings. I, like most others I know, learned early on to become adept at hiding my feelings from others and—with even more disastrous results—hiding them from myself. Dream awareness is the antidote for that sad state of affairs. These pearls of the night are a rich, built-in source of knowledge and an invaluable tool for living "the fully examined life".

This handbook has also been inspired by my participation in a series of Deep Listening ® Retreats facilitated by composer, philosopher Pauline Oliveros at Rose Mountain Retreat Center, high in the Sangre de Cristo Mountains of New Mexico. During these retreats, set amongst rustling Aspen Groves and imposing rock formations, Pauline created strategies for Deep Listening™ for women and men at beginning and advanced levels. Pauline describes her lifelong practice of Deep Listening™ as listening to everything all the time and reminding yourself if you are not listening. Pauline made a ten year commitment to teaching at Rose Mountain between 1991 and 2000. Other Deep Listening Retreats and workshops have taken place and continue throughout the world.

My role in these retreats, at first informally and then formally as I joined Pauline and Tai Chi instructor Heloise Gold as a teacher, was that of "Dream Keeper". At least once a day during a given six day retreat I facilitated dream recall and led dream processes with the group. This served to create a twenty four hour state of Deep Listening for participants.

◆   ◆   ◆

Row, row, row your boat/gently down the stream/merrily, merrily, merrily, merrily/life is but a dream."

Dancing on the Edges of Dreams

There are many systems for understanding dreams, some very new, and many more, quite ancient. To quote international dream teacher Robert Bosnak on the two most well known dream philosophers: "Freud used the images in dreams as mere starting points in a process of free association," C.G. Jung, on the other hand, felt the image itself to be of primary importance."

Jung perceived the dream as an environment, an actual place where we find ourselves and where events occur. He called this environment, "The Reality of the Soul". He wrote, "The dream is the small hidden door in the deepest and most intimate sanctum of the soul, which opens into that primeval cosmic night that was soul long before there was a conscious ego and will be soul far beyond what a conscious ego could ever reach."

Despite the widespread use of Jungian methodology for analyzing dreams, Jung himself did not encourage a set system of dream interpretation. He was respectful of individual dreams; and stated that each dream is its own interpretation!

The great seer Edgar Cayce commented on hundreds of dreams of petitioners, giving them advice on health, past lives, and relationships. He felt that dream recall became easier as his patient's lived more closely in accord with their ideals.

Philosopher Rudolph Steiner felt that our spirituality could directly effect our dream life. He linked spirituality to the arts and once wrote, "The disposition to dreaming makes us poets."

Physicist and psychologist Arnold Mindell's work reveals how dreams become evident in the body as uncontrollable body sensations and subtle communication signals.

As for my own dream philosophy, it is important to state here that "analyzing" dreams in the classical sense is low on my list of priorities. Mostly, I like to think of myself as a Dream Facilitator and a Celebrant of Dreams. I am interested in Dream Community and in inspiring curiosity about dreams. I am interested in empowering others to create their own dream systems.

When working with people privately as a psychotherapist, I focus attention on as many levels of my patient's dreams as I can. (I believe it was the always illuminating psychologist James Hillman who reminded us in a recent work that the word patient stems from the verb "to patient". It is in this context that I use it here.) Indeed, the hard work of those who *patient* in psychotherapy (both the therapist and the one who comes to her for assistance) can yield moments of luminous revelation.

Although I resist labels of all kinds as stubbornly as I can, my work could be called "transpersonal" or "psycho-spiritual". That is to say, I approach each individual from the perspective that she is essentially whole; a part of the "whole" to which we all belong. I call this whole by many names: Spirit, God, goddess, Universe, the Tao, Nzambi, Nana, She Who is Nameless, Great Mystery, Auset, and Maat are but a few of them. We may not know just *what* it is, but most all of us sense (even if it may only be once or twice in our lives) that *something* exists beyond our personal selves. So for me and for my colleagues who hold similar views, there is nothing to be "fixed", nothing inherently wrong, only processes to unfold. Toward this end, I attempt to access the widest range of compassion and knowledge that I can, in support of the person who has come before me.

I pay attention to characters and stories that arise as a part of patients' dreams, and I listen deeply with what I call "full body listening" in order to assess the "edges" which always appear in dream time. Edges are those places in our psyches where we dance with our deepest desires and our deepest fears, where we teeter on the precipice of the future. They are the places at which we pause, pushed by the present, pulled by the past. What will happen to us if we cross over? What will happen to us if we change?

Dreams, being essentially timeless, can show us what it is like to move beyond our present edges.

I once dreamed of a figure walking along the edge of what we perceive as time. "Time" appeared as structured, slotted areas or worlds below him; areas which the large figure could span or enter at will. In the dream, it was clear that time itself was an arbitrary concept. The dream figure could choose any of the slots to inhabit that he wanted or he could choose none. The most important thing for me about this dream was the experiential understanding of the artificial construct of time.

This poem by the Indian Buddhist scholar Nagarjuna, based on his reading of Buddha's Perfection of Wisdom sutras beautifully expresses this concept:

TIME

If I had a past,
What is now and yet to come
Would have already happened.
Were there no now and future then,
How could now and future
Ever have a past?

Without a past
There is no now and future'

What is now and still to come
Would never happen.

Past, present, future
Are like bottom, middle, top
And one, two, three

You can't grasp time
And times you can
Are never time itself
Why configure time you cannot grasp?

If time depends on things,
How could I ever have
Time apart from things?
Without things how could time persist?

While exploring the edges that appear in dreams, I follow with interest my own version of the patient's dream and observe the third dream (primary among many others) that is being "dreamed up" between us in the room. (If you haven't noticed this already, try listening to another person telling you their dream. Notice, that while you are listening, you are imaging or dreaming your own version of their dream. It is a different dream-your own, inspired by theirs. The place where your two dreams meet is a numinous new reality that connects you in dreamtime. If you honor this place, you are in deep communion with the other person.

For me, this is a sacred place. Out of the other "dreamings" in the room, important meanings can emerge for both of us "patients" with some gentle exploration on my part. It is a privilege to be able to show a person the "dream ropes" as it were, and have him take it from there and go on to enjoy his own explorations.

I bring to the work my training in several modalities; my four transformational years of study in the Helix Training Program, with therapists, Lynne Aston, Barbara Crosby, Joan Polvoerde, Naomi Schechter, and Julie Winter. This work included training in body oriented therapies, gestalt therapy, Eriksonian Hypnosis, Buddhist psychology, group dynamics, body oriented therapy and a wide range of metaphysical studies. I studied Clinical Hypnotherapy at a later date with Peter Blum. There were also eight years (some of them concurrent to the Helix Training) in Julie Winter's Healing Classes and eight years of study with Taoist Master T.K. Shih; two years of which were spent in his inaugural training program in Qi Healing for Therapists and Physicians. This work included studying five thousand years of Taoist history, energy practice, healing forms and training in diagnosing problems of the mind, body, and spirit. Master Shih taught us: "The Ocean is big, but the heart is Biggest".

I value the Coma Work and *World Work* Training done with Amy Mindell and Arnold Mindell (founder of Dream Body Work and Process Oriented Psychology); and I am greatly influenced by their philosophies. In addition I attempt to bring to every aspect of my life, the precepts imparted to me by H.E. Tai Situ Rinpoche; H.E. Kalu Rinpoche,. H.E. Jamgun Kontrul, Rinpoche, and H.E. The Dalai Lama.

As my work has deepened, I have explored the ancient mysteries of the world, in particular those of Egypt. For over fifteen years I have conducted trainings in Women's Mysteries (For Women Who Want to Go Deeper ™). In order to provide enough time to develop the sense of community I was interested in fostering, I began to offer year long programs incorporating teachings about women's mores throughout the world with training in ceremony, ritual, oracular forms and altered states. To make a home for this part of my work, I have created The Ministry of Maåt, Inc. a spiritual and educational organization with goals of nurturing world wide harmony.

This book is intended to assist in pointing the way toward deeper dream investigations, while at the same time addressing some common questions and concepts about dreaming, hence the title "handbook".

A look in any good bookstore or library or a perusal of the partial bibliography in the back of this book will turn up enough information to keep an interested researcher occupied for several lifetimes.

I am grateful to the family, friends, students and patients who generously donated dreams and assisted with the production of this handbook. Special thanks to Dr. Richard Corriere for his friendship and dream mentoring—and thanks to members of the Deep Listening Community, The Women's Mysteries Community, The Egyptian Mysteries Community, my mother, Leighla Whipper Ford, my sons, Alessandro Bovoso, Nico Bovoso, and Antonio Bovoso, and my life partner Pauline Oliveros.

◆   ◆   ◆

We are such stuff/as dreams are made on, and our little life/is rounded with a sleep. Shakespeare, The Tempest

Toward A Dream Community

Dream Community is a beautiful thing. We are all automatically members of this community, and we share the dream dimensions whether we are rich or poor, young or old. We dream in Angola and we dream in New York City. We dream in all weathers and through all the varying events and emotions of our lives. We are all dreamers. Because of this, dream sharing is a extraordinarily effective way of *communing* with other humans.

Arnold Mindell, in *The Shaman's Body*, relays the comment of an Australian aborigine he met during his travels, "We dream individually because we share the same dream."

The idea of people simply telling each other their dreams on a regular basis is the most rudimentary form of "Dream Community". All dreams, those that have already occurred, and those yet to come are eligible to be honored; and dreamers living, dead and yet to be born are welcome members of the community.

The ability to honor a dream, its contents, characters and inhabitants for what they are, without imposing a preconceived structure can yield great rewards. It is my hope that as we become more and more used to telling our dreams to each other we will eliminate the need for such common disclaimers as "You're going to think I'm crazy but I had this *weird* dream last night!"

When two or more people are telling each other their dreams, communication automatically takes place on a deep feeling level. When "full body listening" is taking place, it doesn't matter whether the "meaning" of the dream is understood from a logical perspective. Something else important is being transmitted; something palpable that comes through on a body level and on the subtle, non-linear levels of the psyche. Understanding *is* taking place, but it is of a different kind, an especially soul-satisfying kind.

When a rigid structure is imposed on a dream, the dream can become "flattened", its life juices completely squeezed out. Often, to my way of thinking, the dreamer is in danger of losing the gift of her own dream as it becomes the property of another. As brilliant as the dream experts can be, relying solely on the theories of others has limitations. If you give yourself permission to shop around, you may discover that you prefer one method or theory to another, or that a given method seems to fit a certain dream better than another. It can be fascinating to apply more than one method to the same dream. Or, one method can apply at one time in your life, but not another.

Opening up your understanding of dreams to include the concepts of multiple or simultaneous meanings is a way of allowing these precious messages from the psyche to breathe more freely. Once you begin to honor these gifts by paying attention; writing them down in journals, talking about them, telling them to friends and family—the "meanings" of your dreams begin to become clear in an organic way—from the inside out, as it were. A person who has been working with his dreams in this manner, for even a very short while, begins to open to a fuller way of *being* in the world, and ultimately, this latter, is the most important thing of all.

"I dreamt that I dwelt in marble halls/and each damp thing that creeps and crawls/Went wobble-wobble on the walls." Lewis Carroll, From the Palace of Humbug, 1855

THE DREAMER'S DOMAINE

When did we humans begin to lose faith in our dreams? It did not exactly happen from one moment to the next, but began in earnest around the 16th Century, following the recasting of the world in a linear manner and the disavowal of the "invisible" and intangible realms of feelings and dreams.

Carolyn Merchant writes in "The Death of Nature": "….the new world view….by reconceptualizing reality as a machine rather than a living organism, sanctioned the domination of both nature and women. The Contributions of such founding fathers of modern science as Francis Bacon, William Harvey, Rene Descarte, Thomas Hobbes and Issaac Newton must be reevaluated."

Some of the resulting tragedies of the shift in world view include the eradication of millions of women during witch hunts, the decimation of Warlocks, Druids and Aborigines, and the destruction of indigenous peoples on every continent, all of whom lived in a close relationship to their dreams. The year 1592 saw the arrival of the Portuguese on the coast of the Kongo bringing with them the disastrous infiltration of European mercantile values and the beginning of the Diaspora of the peoples of the African continent.

Leonard Shlain, in *The Goddess Vs The Alphabet*, postulates that with the advent of the alphabet in human cultures, the human brain shifted from greater primacy of right brain activity associated with imagery and dreaming to the more linear, left brain activity of writing and reading. Our understanding of ourselves as integral parts of a single dreaming universe was gradually lost, resulting in devaluation of nature and of those who revere nature. It is certainly true that we have gone from the time when a person described as one adept at dreaming was revered, to a time when to be "a dreamer" or one who "lives in a dream world" has an overtly pejorative connotation.

The Dreamer in a community was the person in touch with a wide range of intuitive knowledge—knowledge that was not easily accessible to the average person. The Dreamer had the ability to mediate between worlds, to walk the fine line between "the dream of reality and the reality of the dream. In this manner she was able to understand when danger was near and to assist the well being of the community through messages from the greater dreaming consciousness.

It was dangerous work, for the realms of the underworld need skillful navigation. Decoding night dreams, seeding visions, travelling on shamanic journeys in altered states and having the ability to induce such states in others, were all a part of the Dreamer's Domain. We modern day Deep Dreamers, pulling at the threads that continue to link us to the old ways, are the lineage holders of that domain.

The Twentieth Century saw the advent of Freudian psychology, and witnessed some widely disseminated and often misunderstood concepts associated with dreaming. This caused many to grow self conscious and ashamed and fearful about what unsavory hidden secrets might be revealed by the unconscious! When I have created Dream Festivals-large, sometimes month long city wide events celebrating dreams in as many ways possible, I have found that the politicians with whom I deal tend to be nervous about the theme. Should they associate themselves with dreams in any manner? Of what will the opposite party accuse them? They seem to be weighing the prospect that dreams are downright dangerous, maybe subversive, murky stuff. Of course, it is my vision that one day all the world politicians will tell each other their dreams. Imagine!

Despite the reluctance of the mainstream to respect night dreams as being of great import to individuals or to the society as a whole; the word "dream" itself is frequently used in common parlance. Just listen to any radio station playing popular songs, or check out the names of perfumes, garments and various appliances. The word is used in a modified form that is acceptable. The concept of dream as "something desirable" is retained e.g., a dream boat, a dream ticket, a dream date, etc. "To dream" has also come to mean "to wish". "I dream that I have a brand new convertible!"

When I taught poetry during residencies in New York State and City schools, most kids interpreted the word this way until I explained. The numinous concept of the word is retained in the usage that refers to a great communal vision, as in Martin Luther King's "I have a dream."

Still, the very prevalence of dream themes in our culture indicates an underlying yearning, a kind of nostalgia perhaps, for the unifying collective dream realms once so familiar to our ancestors.

> *"Orestes: Did you ask what the dream was? Can you describe it clearly?" From The Choephori c.460 BC Aeschylus*

PAYING ATTENTION

As elusive as they may seem, dreams are also amazingly responsive. For example, simply because you have read this far in this handbook, your dreams are already gathering, waiting to make themselves known to you in new ways. It is up to you to determine what kind of new relationship you would like to cultivate with your dreams. If you pay attention, call them to you, make a place for them, nurture them, they will come to you. Whether you simply talk about them, think about them, or keep ongoing dream journals, they can respond by feeding your soul with delectable tidbits-from subtle sensations to sumptuous symbols that practically hit you over the head with their 'meanings'. Or you may be privy to comical and blatant set ups and puns that have you howling with laughter. The humor of dreams is perhaps the one thing that the uninitiated find most surprising.

We tend to take ourselves quite seriously, and it can be eye opening to discover that our dreams can be considerably more light hearted than we. Sometimes they can be downright irreverent, like a wise and maddening friend who is none the less well loved. Perhaps "friend" is the optimal word here, for your dreams can be cherished friends, confidantes, teachers—You can come to think of them as a respected part of yourself, ready to supply you with a constant stream of insights into your deepest nature. Because of this they can supply you as well with insights into the deepest nature of the universe.

> *That we come to this earth to live is untrue. We come but to sleep, to dream.*—*Aztec Poem, Anonymous*

Who Dreams?

In 1953, researchers discovered a stage of sleep called REM, for rapid eye movement. During REM sleep much of the brain becomes as active as it is during waking. The eyes dart around behind closed lids as if following an action-packed sporting event. People awakened from REM sleep almost always say they have been dreaming. That led researchers to equate REM sleep with dreaming.

But recent research has shown that REM sleep is not the exclusive province of dreams. Although most dreams happen then, people also dream at other times during sleep.

"REM sleep is the best place for dreaming," says Ernest Hartmann, a professor of psychiatry at Tufts University in Boston. "It is not the only place."

Everyone dreams, even though we may not remember. Humans dream approximately 100 minutes per sleep period. The dreams most remembered are those that occur toward morning. Based upon the link between REM sleep and dreams; it has been shown that babies probably dream in the womb. The dream state has been observed in warm blooded animals (birds and mammals) but no one has yet been able to record such a state in fish, amphibians or reptiles, with the possible exception of the crocodile. Both chickens and cows dream 25 minutes each day while chimpanzees are close to humans with ninety minutes of dreaming per day. The most active dreamer is the domestic cat who dreams 200 minutes per day.

Controversial theories about the nature of sleep and the purpose of dreaming abound, but one of the most intriguing is that of pioneering French sleep and dream researcher Dr. Michel Jouvet, who postulates that we need regular, periodic dreaming to preserve our very individuality, and that dreaming is a time for *essential genetic reprogramming* within the brain.

> *I want to keep my dreams, even bad ones, because without them, I might have nothing all night long."* Joseph Heller, Something Happened, 1974

I Never Remember My Dreams

I am always fascinated when a participant in one of my workshops claims that she *never dreams*.

This is often said proudly and maybe even defiantly. Somehow in the next few sentences with a little encouragement on my part, a dream usually spills forth from her lips. The speaker may reluctantly and somewhat sheepishly admit that, yes, that *was* a dream. Over time I have discovered that the reasons for the statement are various. In some cases the dreamer expects a full story and not a part of a story. In other cases, strange as it may seem, the dream realms are so subtle, or some people have grown so used to devaluing such states that they just don't recognize them. Of course, not remembering can also be a form of self protection. Individuals who have experienced past trauma and who fear that trauma's surfacing, often completely suppress their dream recall. There are also some medications that inhibit dreaming.

> *"There's nothing wrong with nightmares," Hungry Joe answered,*
> *"everybody has nightmares." Joseph Heller, Catch 22, 1962*

Nightmares Give Way To The Light

In the most severe cases of trauma, such as when early abuse has occurred to the dreamer, or is suspected, it is strongly recommended that a skilled therapist assist in moving through recall. There is no need to hurry memories. In these cases, we can honor the timing of dream revelations, and even suggest to our dreams that we not be given information that we are not ready to receive and process.

A participant in a workshop I was giving at Esalen Institute in Big Sur had not remembered any dreams since she began to have memories of a very traumatic time in her life. During the course of the workshop, she began to feel safe enough to let a dream come to her.

"I feel as though I'm ready now." she told me. Her remembered dream was gentle and informative and the good feelings it contained confirmed that she was on her way to healing from the early difficulty. She came into the group on the last morning positively shining.

"I feel as if I've gotten a large part of myself back." She told the group.

Defusing frightening dreams is generally healthier than *stuffing* them. Pushing down such material can actually serve to make it more dense, giving it more power. (This could be called "the volcano effect". When the capstone is off, and the lava is flowing bit by bit, the danger of a full explosion in minimized.) By writing the troubling dream down, talking with a therapist or a friend, practicing waking imagination to shift the events in the dream, the dream can gradually lose its power over us and healing can begin.

"Oh, I've had such a curious dream!" said Alice. Lewis Carroll, Alice's Adventures in Wonderland, 1865

Making a Place for Dreams

If you begin to keep a Dream Journal and leave a little quiet time for recording notes about your dreams each morning, they will arrive. Try eliminating strident alarm clocks that buzz, blip and beep! Try instead, waking up to music or tapes with a radio/cassette/CD clock. If you want to be really innovative, you can also record your own supportive messages to your dreaming self or (your waking self for that matter.) Another important thing: once awake, try not jumping straight up out of bed. *Allow enough extra time* (just five or ten minutes will do) to let your head sink back on the pillow. Don't force it. Just be receptive—this will make space for fading dreams to float back up to the surface. Then be sure to jot them down before heading into the rest of your day. If memory recall has not yet occurred, you can also remain open to receiving the dream content later on. Something may occur during the day that will bring the memory of the entire dream flooding back. Sometimes just bending over to pick up something in the shower will do it. (The rush of blood to the memory storage place in the brain could be the reason why this one works.)

> *"Dreams are the touchstones of our characters." H.D. Thoreau, A Week on the Concord and Merrimack Rivers, 1849*

Dream Fragments Are Whole Dreams

Dream Fragments count as dreams because dreams are *holographic*. In the smallest fragment, we are able to receive information of as much relevance as the most involved and complete dream story. For example, last night I dreamed quite simply of a pen called a Forca Pen. (Pronounced in what I eventually realized was the Brazilian Portuguese way-Forze-a) If there was more to the dream, I couldn't remember a bit of it, but I could see the pen and I knew that it was a very special brand of pen that I was going to get. A great feeling of happiness and satisfaction came over me at the understanding that I would get myself such an object. I could even see the "familiar" logo of this famous pen. On waking I still had the good feeling and gradually realized that the Forca Pen was not (to my knowledge) a brand name in the waking world. I feel that the dream was speaking to me of power (force a!) and the pen felt like a potent symbol of my writing. Concentrating more on the power of my pen (without *forcing* it) would give me the good feeling that I had in the dream. A clear direction was being pointed out to me by a simple fragment.

"There is no such thing as a small dream, only small dream perspective." Stephen A. Martin, Smaller than Small, Bigger than Big"

The Dreamer Knows Best

According to noted dream theorist Jeremy Taylor, each dream carries at least one message with new information for the dreamer. Remember though, that although one meaning may stand out for you, your dream can be understood on many levels.

The ultimate "meaning" of any dream belongs to the dreamer herself, no matter what good ideas another may have on the subject. A Deep Dream Listener, opens to receive her friend's dream from a whole body perspective. This means temporarily suspending the mind's tendency to want to show how clever it is—to jump on a "meaning" to analyze, to ponder, to squelch—in short to proclaim a kind of dominance over the other's dream. I recommend beginning dream discussions with" If this were my dream, I'd imagine this is what it was telling me—"Or, in my version of your dream, I see."

"Our truest life is when we are in dreams awake." H.D. Thoreau, A Week on the Concord and Merrimack Rivers, 1849

Tell your dream in the present tense

Use the present tense when writing in the journal and when dream sharing. This proves difficult for some at the beginning, but it becomes quickly apparent that the dream breathes its truth with greater ease in this manner. Whether the dream occurred last night, or years ago, it still has the ability to evoke powerful feelings in the dreamer. The mind, unable to create the artificial separation that the past tense implies, begins to understand the current pertinence of the dream material with greater ease.

> The Chinese sage Chaung-tsu dreamed he was a butterfly and on waking wondered whether he then had been a man dreaming, or might not now be a butterfly dreaming it was a man.

Waking Up In the Dream

Many of the world's religions and philosophies consider dream awareness an important means to awakening our spiritual selves. Through understanding the nature of dreaming, we begin to understand the dream-like quality of waking and thus begin to cling less to material things. Sogyal Rinpoche explains the importance of meditation and of realizing the illusory nature of consensus reality in *The Tibetan Book of Living and Dying*, he states, "What is essential—is to realize now, in life when we still have a body, that its apparent, so convincing solidity is a mere illusion." (We must) like the "child of illusion" see directly, as we do in meditation that all phenomena are illusory and dream-like."

According to many Buddhist teachings, consciousness and awareness that we are dreaming is a time honored practice for learning how to maintain awareness after death.

Tenzing Wangyal Rinpoche in *The Tibetan Yogas of Dream and Sleep,* speaks of three levels of dreaming that form a progression in dream practice: Ordinary Dreams, Dreams of Clarity and Clear Light Dreams. He outlines a detailed method for dream study which requires dedicated practice in order to attain proficiency. Namkhai Norbu Rinpoche in *Dream Yoga and the Practice of Natu-*

ral Light, states that in the Djogchen system of Buddhism, it is not necessary to commit oneself to working on dreams. Lucidity arises naturally out of the practice of the natural light. The Natural Light arises at a moment when the mind is not functioning, between falling asleep and just prior to the onset of dreaming.

Lama Surya Das in *Tibetan Dream Yoga* speaks of the dream state as "Fourth Time" a malleable realm where the past, present and future meet.

His Holiness The Dalai Lama indicates that the three crucial life stages of dying, the Bardo, (the in-between state between death and rebirth) and conception are analogues to the states of falling asleep, the dream state, and then waking. He outlines in *Sleeping, Dreaming and Dying,* practices which can lead one to achieve the state of lucidity in dreams. Meditation, visualization practices, diet, time of sleep and depth of sleep are but a few aspects of these profound spiritual practices. Importantly, the first step is "to recognize the dream as the dream."

Toward this end, researcher, Stephen La Berge, has evolved extensive techniques, including a Dream Mask with sensors and a small signaling light that alert the dreamer at the onset of REM sleep, the rapid eye movement that signals onset of most of our dreaming. La Berge suggests in his seminal work, *Lucid Dreaming,* that we ask ourselves periodically during the day, "Is this a Dream?" The idea is to carry this over into your dreams in order to "wake up in the dream". My own variation on this suggestion is to try repeating periodically, "This is a Dream!" both during "waking" and "sleeping".

La Berge writes, "If you keep the mind sufficiently active while the tendency to enter REM sleep is strong, you feel your body fall asleep, but you, that is to say your consciousness, remains awake. The next thing you know, you will find yourself in the dream world, fully lucid."

The pliant place "in between" waking and sleeping, termed "The Hypnogogic State", is experienced either heading into sleep, or coming up out of sleep. Dream Researchers have found this to be a time when psychic abilities are at their highest. Targeted messages were transmitted and received during this state with great success in Montague Ullman's Dream Lab Experiments in the 1960s. In this state, many find it easy to slip back into a dream and continue where they left off, or to slip back into a dream and re-dream a dream in a more satisfactory manner then the first time.

Lucid dreams are often bright and luminous in color and tone. They actually *feel* good to the dreamer and the effect is lasting long after the dreamer has truly awakened to this reality. Studies have shown that such dreams are actually physically good for us—that good feeling endorphins are released into the body that give us a decided boost for several days.

One way of achieving lucidity involves giving yourself a prearranged signal before going to sleep. Try the well known method (given to Carlos Castenda by the shaman *Don Juan*) of noticing your *hands* in your dream. Your hands then become the signal to recognize that you are dreaming, and the next step is to "wake up" further inside of your dream. Or you may simply seek out incongruities in the dream "field" alerting you to the fact that you are dreaming, e.g., a talking animal, or a lamp post standing in the center of your living room floor! One good test as to whether or not you are dreaming or awake is to attempt to lift up off the ground and fly. How often I have been absolutely certain I was not inside of a dream, looking around cautiously, touching things, saying to myself, "Now, this is definitely, *real.* I know this is real!" only to discover on testing it out that I could fly down several flights of stairs, or float up to the ceiling.

When you find yourself awake inside a dream, try to maintain the dream state. This can take practice, as excited dreamers can find themselves suddenly popping out of the dream entirely. Many dreamers tell me that they are able to recognize they are dreaming in the middle of a nightmare, enough so that they can wake themselves up from it. I tell them they are already practicing for the lucid state. The next step after the recognition is to stay inside the dream and to transform what is happening into something far more harmonious. (You will find various methods of stabilizing awareness in the reading materials.) Next begin your explorations of the dream world. The options are seemingly limitless. Become powerful. Visit an important place or person. Further your spiritual life by seeking the company of high spiritual teachers, known or unknown. As with all your dreaming, it is fun as well as rewarding to keep good records of your lucid dream experiences

Still, it can be sobering to remember that even for the advanced spiritual practitioner of dreaming, attachments of all kinds, even to the content of our dreams are eventually left behind. Great teachers report that when awareness becomes absolute, dreams cease completely-to be replaced by an indescribable luminous clarity.

"There is a dream dreaming us." A Kalahari Bushman

World Wide Dreaming

The Iroquois:

This advanced North American culture, (sometimes known as the Ho-de-no-sau-nee or the People of the Long House) created a Confederacy of interdependent allied nations which was the inspiration for the formation of the United States of America. The Iroquois believed that we all have a Dreaming Soul. It was understood that every dream contained a divine message. The diety Tarengawagon was much revered, for he was the sender of dreams. They held large Dream Festivals called Honnonouaroia during which dream guessing games were played. These games were observed and commented upon in the 17th Century by Jesuit priests. Some commentators were repulsed and mystified by the wild carnival type antics; while others were fascinated and impressed by what they considered to be the 'sophistication' of the some of the Iroquois dream practices. These included a kind of confessional during which dreamers told their dreams and received counseling from experts.

During the Dream Festivals, participants presented their dreams to the gathered crowds using mime and riddles. Sometimes they ran from dwelling to dwelling insisting that their dream be guessed or somehow gratified. The onlookers then did their best to *guess* the chosen dreamer's dream. It was very bad form and sometimes dangerous not to guess what the dreamer's Dream Soul wanted.

(There are accounts of dwelling places set on fire!) Once guessed, the person was given what their dreaming soul needed, either symbolically or actually. A rare flower high in the hills might be sought for the dreamer, or standard monogamous customs might be broken if it turned out, that *this* was what a Dream Soul desired. Dreaming practices of many kinds continue to be an integral feature of Native American cultures in this country.

Egypt:

Many are familiar with Biblical references to dreams and dreaming as a means of communication with God. Jacob's dream which fore-told coming events in Egypt is well known. The Pharaoh Thutmose IV (1400 BC) having fallen asleep in the shadow of the Sphinx, received important dream communications which led him to remove the sands that had covered up the lower sections of the ancient monument. Once the sands were removed, he recorded his dream on a pillar located between the paws of the Sphinx. The ancient (reconstructed) words can be viewed there today.

The ancient Egyptians had dream temples in which priests and priestesses were able to dream healing dreams for petitioners. There was an important Dream Temple at Denderah, at the Temple of Hathor, as well as one at Memphis where Serapis, a dream diety, was worshiped. The oldest known temple was at the Step Pyramid in Saqqara. This magnificent pyramid complex was designed for King Netjerykhe Djoser by architect/physician/magician and astrol-oger Imhotep. Imhotep would become the only human being dei-fied by later generations of Egyptians.

Today, the beautiful causeways, colonnades and walls of Saqqara are being reconstructed by dedicated French archeologist, Professor Jean Pierre-Lauer. Lauer, who began his work in 1937 and is now in his late 90s, is still working on his enormous life project. I have had the privilege of conversing with this remarkable man at Saqqara three times over the past 20 years. During my visit in 1999, he gra-ciously accepted the admiring attentions of visitors and after they had drifted on, spoke lovingly of his years at the Saqqara complex, culminating in his current concentration on the small chapels in the sed-festival court. Later, I watched from the causeway above as Lauer, wearing his characteristic sun shading cotton hat, and cool cotton shirt and pants, accompanied by an Egyptian foreman in a flowing gallabaya, slowly crossed the open courtyard. He was on his way to oversee the continuous and painstaking work of his crew. I had a sudden realization: Lauer is a modern day Imhotep, carrying the work of the great magician into the Twenty First Century.

> *"—I saw my favourite trees step out and promenade up, down and around, very curiously-with a whisper from one, leaning down as he pass'd me; We do all this on the present occasion, exceptionally, just for you."* Walt Whitman, *"Thoughts Under an Oak,",* From *Speciment Days 1875*

Indian Upanishads

These sacred texts, dating from the first millennium BC outline the contrasting states of consciousness of waking and dreaming; known respectively as Vaisvanara, meaning Common to All Men, and Taijasa, "originating from and consisting of tejas ('light')." They are also identified with the first and second elements of the sacred sylla-ble AUM or OM (a and u being pronounced together in Sanskrit as *o.* The concluding element, M, is identified with the state of deep, dreamless sleep. The text describes four conditions of The Self (Atman): The Waking State, The Dreaming State, The Deep Sleep State and the Transcendent State (unsounded, beyond action and blissful) of non phenomenal existence. In terms of sound, this fourth condition represents the silence before, after and supporting the sounding of the syllable OM.

The Senoi

Until they were interfered with by outsiders, the Senoi of Malaysia, were reportedly an extraordinarily peaceful people with no word for war in their language. They told their dreams in their dwelling places each morning. They, like the Achuar, a community of dream-ers currently living in South America, were adept at listening to the dreams of the community. In this manner they always had their pulse on the needs of the people. If a child or an adult needed some-thing, all would know about it through listening to their dreams. If the community as a whole needed to move on from one place to another, it would become apparent through the dreams of the group.

Among the Senoi, the children were taught to interact with their dreams and were able to transform dangerous animals, or enemies into harmless figures, and to call for a dream helper when they needed to. Among older community members, dream lovers were to be honored, no matter who they were and not only was it suggested that one move through to orgasm in the dream; it was recom-mended that a gift be requested of the lover. This gift could be received in the dream itself or in waking state. Arnold Mindell has noted that the Senoi had a ritual in which *any* person who appeared in a dream would be entitled to receive a gift by the dreamer.

He suggests that the Senoi understood that when we are dream-ing of another we are in a sense "taking something from them" unless we own our projection of them and recognize that they (and their qualities) are not entirely separate from ourselves.

Three Other Dream Customs:

The Masai of Kenya do not wake a sleeper suddenly for fear that her wandering spirit may not be able to reenter the body.

The Fellahs of the Nile Delta envelop their heads with a turban to prevent the escape of the soul through the top of the head during sleep.

In 16th Century Ndongo, the country now known as Angola, Njinga Mbandi (1592–1620), the female ruler who ruled as king of the Mbundu people, kept the invading Portuguese at bay for forty years. She received instructions and assistance from the former King (Ngola's) bones through dreams and visions.

Sacred Sites:

Sleeping at Sacred Sites has been an important tradition of the peoples of many lands, including the Celts, who were particularly in tune with places of power and the ley lines of the earth that connect them. Throughout the world, the purpose of seeking out and sleeping at such sites is to obtain a special vision or dream of revelation and healing, containing a message, a direction. Most of the ancient churches and cathedrals of England and Europe are built upon such sacred sites.

The Step pyramid at Saqqara became a popular site for pilgrimages by pious Greeks for centuries after the reign of King Djozer and his magician/architect, Imhotep. For those who *patiented* at the site, the god of healing was said to appear in dreams in the form of a snake or a black dog. Imhotep later became associated with Aesculepius, the Greek God of Healing, and the Greeks continued the tradition of Dream Healing sites and Temples.

The most famous shrine to Aesculepius was created at Epidaurus in the fifth century BC In order for any new site to be affiliated with the main temple, a sacred snake from Epidaurus was ritually transported and installed there. Greek paintings of Aesculepius, often feature a dog, as well as the snakes of the Caduceus he holds. Both symbols are holdovers from more ancient Egyptian traditions and the cult of Imhotep. (The intertwined snakes are still a symbol of healing—a part of the American Medical Association's famous logo.)

The earliest Greek Temples, deriving from the Egyptian practices, furthered the concept of a real god making a tangible visit in a recognizable physical form. Descriptions of the morning scene in such temples include the specter of live snakes crawling about, bloody remnants of various operations having taken place during the night, and groggy memories of participants who tell of encounters with the healing god during the night.

In *Prometheus Bound* by Aeschylus, Dream Interpretation, or oneiromancy (based on the Greek word for dream *oneiros*) is evoked as one of the most important signs of civilization. Prometheus declares himself to be the major teacher of the art. Primary among the later philosophers, Aristotle wrote three books on dreams, and stated, "The most skillful interpreter of dreams is he who has the faculty of observing resemblances."

Creating Your Private Dream Temple

As we have seen, above, the early Dream Temples proliferated in ancient Egypt and later, in Greece. Dreamers also fervently consulted their dreams at home. The methods of receiving information were numerous, but all involved getting the answer in a dream and the later interpretation of the received information. Incubation spells were numerous among the Egyptians and the Greeks. A typical spell would have involved dipping a reed in myrrh or another special substance and writing on clean papyrus.

(Some spells were written on reeds.) Incense might be burned, and the space and dreamer herself would be purified by applying special essential oils. The Papyrus might then be placed under a lamp or under a pillow. Certain phrases would be repeated a certain number of times-three or seven were popular-then a diety would be invoked to oversee her dream request.

This ancient system adapts well to our modern times.

I love the concept of the Dream Temple, and often give this title to my workshops for those who are interested in this aspect of dreaming. You could begin to think of your own bedroom as a Dream Temple, starting by clearing away elements in the room that distract and fill you with worldly concern. You could also imagine benevolent beings around you. Or, perhaps just thinking of a beloved grandmother, or reading soothing words before sleep would be enough.

Filling the room and your mind with thoughts that represent the best of what you want for yourself and the world, can assist in getting a better night's sleep and while you're at it, having wonderful harmonious dreams.

In many Native traditions a creative endeavor is always *dreamed* before it is created in this reality. Many artists use their dreams as inspiration for new work and they often help artists to break through creative blocks. Remember, dreams are our deepest source of creativity. During the night many avid dreamers receive answers to tough problems, or find new creative resources that enhance their lives. Writer Gore Vidal recently mentioned that he always works early in the morning, close to his dreams.

Incubating a dream is easy–and in some way I believe we are always incubating dreams, although due to worldly concerns we may not notice either the questions or the replies. Here is an example of a spontaneous incubation:.

Harrison Ryker, a violinist and composer, told me the following dream experience while we were having dinner in a Hong Kong restaurant this winter:

Around 1971, while working at Hope College, I came across Haydn's wonderful Symphony No. 86 and decided to try it with the college chamber orchestra. When the parts arrived we began sight reading it, and all went fairly well until the finale, where the rhythms of the opening theme tied the string players in knots. When I tried it myself on the violin, I was unable to find a graceful or workable bowing. After some days of fretting over this, I woke up one night having dreamed a bowing for this passage, and then went back to sleep again. Usually when I interrupt a dream in this way, I cannot recall it later. This time, however, it was still on my mind when I woke up in the morning. I scribbled it down on scratch paper, tried it later in the day on the violin, and it worked perfectly. It also worked for the student string players, and we used it in several successful performances."

Sometimes the answers to our questions seem to come unbidden, as in Harrison's musical dream solution. Here's how to do it more consciously. Write out your question, and everything that comes to mind about it about a half an hour to ten minutes before going to sleep, then reduce the whole thing to one succinct sentence. Then write this sentence on a small piece of paper and place it under your pillow. Other dream "anchors" of your choice may be placed close to or on the bed. Dream pillows filled with special herbs have been used by many of my students. Even a special scent could be a powerful anchor. The ancients, notably the Egyptians and the Chinese, used essential oils for purification and healing in sacred ceremonies. Certain herbs like lavender and mugwort have been used both externally as oils or incense and internally as scents and infusions to help bring dreams in. If your anchor is a larger object unsuitable for slipping under your pillow, it can be placed on a bedside table. In the morning jot down any notes that come up. Many will get an answer immediately, but give yourself a good week of dreaming. Telling the dream to a good dream listener or in a dream circle can help unfold the meaning of your dream reply.

Frequently we are unable to see the results of our dream incubation because the linear mind is seeking a linear kind of answer. A first response is often, "I didn't get an answer!" or "I didn't get anything!"

Give the dreams a bit of space and remember, you are not demanding an answer, after all, you are seeking guidance. Try telling the dream to a friend who may be able to see correlations that are opaque to you. Be careful not to ask too broad a question. Some years back, Sally, a student in my dream group, insisted that her dream incubation had not worked. It turned out she had asked the question; "Who am I?"

"So what did you dream?" we asked her.

"All night long, I just kept hearing my answering machine going off over and over, saying, "Hello, this is Sally Kaplan, Hello, this is Sally Kaplan, Hello, this is Sally Kaplan."

Before she'd finished speaking she began to laugh with the rest of us as she realized how the dream had playfully taken her quite literally.

Psychic Communications

A psychic connection between family members is very common. Often mothers know when their children are in danger, or a sister may know when her brother is in need of help. Dreams are the easiest way for most of us to recognize such intimations. We are always receiving psychic information, but due to the constant distractions of our lives, and the lack of training from childhood to recognize and value such messages, most of us tend to miss them.

My grandmother and I had a particularly strong psychic connection, and through my dreams I often knew how she was doing. As I dreamed in my New York loft, she appeared, asking for water. On awakening, I immediately called her in Saratoga where she was living alone, and learned she had fever and needed assistance.

Many friends have told me of communication with loved ones and friends who have passed away. Often the time of death of a relative or a famous person makes itself known in a dream. I was at a gathering in Houston recently when the topic turned to dreams. A few moments before leaving the party, the poet Sekou Karanje recounted the following story:

"I dreamed that I was on a beautiful beach. I looked up and suddenly saw a large black limousine approaching on the sand. It was surrounded by a strange mist with an odd vibration to it. I was disturbed by it. The limo whizzed past me and as it did, the mist was lifting from it. It continued on and sank into the ocean. I then heard words spoken by a Jamaican stewardess friend who was with me.

'That was Bob Marley passing'

"Later that day, I was floored to find out that Marley had passed away around the same time as the dream. I've never had a dream experience like that before. Never!"

The Great prophet and seer Edgar Cayce indicated that many dreams of those who have died are actual "Visitation Dreams" while some are merely projections of thoughts and feelings about the person. Actual visitations make themselves known by the *feeling tone* of the dream. The dreamer herself can come to distinguish between the two kinds of dreams.

Patricia Garfield's book *The Dream Messenger ; How Dreams of the Departed Bring Healing Gifts.* details many aspects of dreams of the dead. Garfield shows how those separated from their loved ones by death can often complete unfinished issues between them in dreams, receiving a sense of completion and consequently, an easing of the grieving process.

Joe Catalano was a beloved member of the community and a composer of extraordinary works evoking our intimate connections with the earth, rivers, and stars. Composer and cellist Anne Bourne, a member of the Deep Listening community, was in deep meditation in Toronto when she received a strong feeling of Joe Later she would learn that the long message and vision that unfolded had come to her at the very moment of his passing. She wrote down her visual impressions, commenting on Joe's words, a small but powerful portion of which I reproduce here:

"Just flow in the river, as part of the river," (I see a wide mouth, a bay, a widening of a body of water…water rising in the air). "When you think you're at the end, you're at the beginning again."

(Clouds rising over the mountains, mist, teardrops of rain, the source.) "*And then you are back in the river again, which means you haven't really gone anywhere, so you don't need to do as much as just flow, be the river, let the river be for you, of you.*"

Five months after Joe's passing, his wife, poet Wendy Burch had the following dream, one of a series:

Dreamed all night of Joe. At first we were walking out onto the Golden Gate Bridge, we thought, but then found that we were on a bridge that suddenly came to an end. Then we were on a ship together, and at some time someone was negotiating with someone else about a law suit regarding a shipwreck. It seemed weak and inconsequential. Joe and I spent so much time together, loving one another. He conveyed to me without words that he loved me forever, that the death, the "twins" (brain tumors), were unreal. We stared at one another and I saw every detail of his face, I saw him clearly and perfectly, and couldn't take my eyes off of him, I looked at him with so much love in me and we held one another every chance we had. We were so happy to be together. At one point we were with others on this ship, and I said, let's make this a lucid dream and we can cure your illness. So I said out loud, 'This is a dream.'

Things seemed clearer, but it was as if we had already been lucid dreaming, just seeing one another and being together, touching one another so vividly. I was completely happy. The dreams went on all night."

Communication With the Future

As we have noted earlier, Dreams are essentially timeless, giving us sporadic access to past, present and future. Through keeping a fairly regular dream journal over a period of a year or more, many dream-

ers are able to observe how dreams forecast events in their lives Precognitive information shows up on a daily basis. Usually the
precognitive information we catch is nothing more startling than
say, dreaming of a red car and then seeing a very similar car the
moment you walk out your door. But sometimes it is more important.

Here is Laura Donnelly's dream, followed by her later journal
entry.

Staten Island, NY October, 1988

> *"I am in an old book store or library standing in front of a book
> rack. The shelves are full of books. I notice especially the books about
> Egypt. A reference person looks something up, reads a quote to me,
> and then gives me the book so I can continue to look for more infor-
> mation. The passage is like a verse in the bible with a number in
> front of it. There are lots of page numbers listed to refer to for more
> information. (210, 437, etc.) It says, 'The lion is the symbol of eter-
> nal life. You will meet your lion-heart in the desert…'*

Some months later, Laura recorded the following:

Egypt, December, 1988

*"At the end of our first day in Egypt our guide takes us to the great pyra-
mids at Giza. We drive out into the desert in order to view the spectacu-
lar site from a distance. Several of us escape from the tour bus and begin
to run down the mountains of sand toward the pyramids. Halfway
down the sandy slope I kick a huge rock. I stop to inspect it. As I am
bending down to pick it up I notice another smaller rock…it is black,*

not sand colored, with sharp edges and shaped perfectly like a heart…it is my lion heart…I found it in the desert."

Evageline Johns' dream at Rose Mountain involves another kind of future break through:

The Dream: July 20 1999:

"I am leading the tribe, single file, up the path, through the woods. We come to a small bridge about six feet across. The leader has to be able to jump across. I just make it. Now we are in my tent. I know its my tent because it has green rim all the way around. I look out and see Jerry looking in at me. I think, "Jerry is an Ogalaw. He has strong magic. If I leave the tent, he will be the leader." I feel anxious, but I do leave the tent. When I step out, it is bright day light and I am in the circular dirt excavation inside of which is a swimming pool. On the other side there are rickety wooden steps leading up and away from the area. There is a beautiful young Afro-American man standing by the pool. I realize that this man is the leader of the tribe. He smiles a warm, friendly smile that makes me feel good down to my toes. He says, "See you tomorrow" and I understand that we are making a film. I walk around the pool to the steps, climb up and leave the dream."

The Waking World: July 21, 1999
"In the morning we start on our morning meditation walk. We have not gone far when our leader, Heloise Gold, stops us. There are about five people ahead of me. She points up the path. There is a fine skunk, fat and silvery with tail held high, walking on the path ahead of us. As we watch the skunk crosses a raised layer of rock which looks like a small bridge from where I stand and disappears into the woods. I am pro-foundly affected. I need to say that my totem (spirit) guide is the skunk,

a fact I discovered earlier this year, before I knew this place of Deep Listening in the Sangre de Cristo Mountains of New Mexico existed. About six months before I had dreamt I found a skunk in my kitchen. I liked it and felt happy to have it there. I drew the skunk from a deck of Medicine cards at my friend Peggy's house. The skunk represents REPUTATION. Respect for yourself and others. This is the message that came through loud and clear as I witnessed the appearance of the skunk:: 'You are on the right path. Trust me.'

kk Later in the week I was invited to participate in a film on the mountain."

Remember, *important* precognitive dreams have their *own special feeling quality.* But even dreams without this special quality can be meaningful. If you dream of a flat tire, it wouldn't hurt to check the tires on your car. Or if you dream a friend is crying, while the dream may have a relationship to your own life and issues, there is no harm in contacting that friend to find out what's up, while being careful not to alarm him, or to lord it over him with your own special knowledge.

For example, it is inappropriate to behave as one psychic but rather immature young man did. After receiving what he thought were dream messages from an acquaintance's grandmother, he attempted to influence his friend's actions with the information he'd gathered. He was puzzled when his friend was angered and began to shun him.

No matter what a dream might indicate to us, it is wise to refrain from carrying out any action that feels immoral, unhealthy, or unethical to your waking self.

The Stuff of Dreams

Body Messages

We can receive messages about physical symptoms from our dreams. They can signal what the body needs in the way of medicine, nourishment, exercise, etc. We can receive information about illness or health. Patricia Garfield's extensive research on body symptoms is detailed in *"Women's Bodies, Women's Dreams.* She writes: "Women who are able to turn to their dreams for nourishment, understanding and guidance often find that the menopausal stage brings dreams of staggering impact. In addition to dreams reflecting their physical symptoms and changing conditions, such women discover an inner transformation unfolding at this stage of life."

Deep Listener composer/pianist and Professor of Music, Janet Hammock made a discovery of her own when she began Hormone Replacement Therapy.

Janet had experienced dwindling dreams during the previous years, and so welcomed a new richness in this area reflecting the body changes she had been experiencing:

"The head of my university music department who is a fine pianist has a grand piano at school which is apparently missing some important internal parts. He really needs those parts! So the piano technician comes to my house and carts my piano off so that he can take from it the parts that Edmund needs for his piano and put them into it. Originally, the technician was going to order the parts for Edmund's instrument, but Edmund needed them right away, so the technician decided to come and take my piano away so he could remove the parts from it and insert them into Edmund's piano! I have no particular feeling about, or reaction to, this. That's the way it is. I go to the university music department

to see Edmund's piano prior to the installation of the needed parts. It is in a room all by itself. It has absolutely no insides at all! There is no keyboard, no legs, no lid. It is an empty shell of wood—essentially the wood frame and sound board only. Furthermore, the piano is upended—the rounded far end of the frame is leaning high up against a wall while the keyboard end (without a keyboard-even it is gone!) is resting on the wooden floor. The piano has a wonderfully airy look to it. I can see the beautiful wallpaper through the inside of the piano! There is nothing else in the room, just this large, dark-wooden, airy empty shell of a piano and the pretty wallpaper which is a wonderful shade of green with swirls of darker green vines and small flowers on it. There is a lovely fresh air breeze blowing through the room from open windows which I cannot see. I awoke feeling terrific!"

Janet wrote, "Upon rereading this dream, Ione, I am again struck by its beauty and the many different ways it may be interpreted, all of which make sense to me".

Children and Animals

Our relationships to babies and animals in dreams can help us to understand our own vulnerabilities as well as the needs of our younger selves. The way we treat little beings or dependent beings in our dreams can be very telling. Dreams of having a baby or an animal and suddenly realizing one has forgotten to feed it are common. Dreams of pregnancy and giving birth are often harbingers of a new persona arriving, a new part of the dreaming announcing itself. Naturally, they can also forecast an actual willingness on the part of the dreamer to give birth in waking state.

One friend who had no conscious thoughts of giving birth had a bountiful dream of herself with full and overflowing breasts nursing two infants. Approximately one year later, she met the man she would marry, a man with a child. She completed the dream by giving birth to another.

I added the category of "Grandbaby Dreams" to my journal with one of my own favorites entitled "Buddha Baby" in which I found a sweet golden brown baby in my office. The dream turned out to be a harbinger of a new grandchild, Mateo, who bore a strong resemblance to the dream infant.

A recently relayed "giving birth "dream shows yet another kind of baby dream: Terry dreamed of giving birth while lying next to her lover, only to have the baby begin to grow at a rapid pace. She discovered that the umbilical cord was still attached. As she explored the dream in waking state, she recognized the feelings she'd been having toward her lover. She actually felt rather *motherly* toward him. She realized she truly wanted to "cut the cord" in order to allow them both to find a more mature relationship.

Futurist and world traveler, Pauline Oliveros sent me her "Turn of the Century" dream which features another kind of growing baby:

"Last night I had a New Year dream:

I was on my way to catch a plane. There was a wild ride to an airport. At one point the driver was going backwards. We arrived. I got out with one shoe missing. I retrieved the Birkenstock from the van and put it on. The path to the terminal was steep and muddy. I started up the path and one leg sank up to my thigh in mud. I then found my way to the side of the path where it was dry.

I climbed to the terminal and went inside. There was an empty room with a baby sitting up on the floor. He was whimpering slightly. He looked at me and began to talk like an adult. He said that they needed some money among other things. I offered him $100. He smiled at me radiantly. I could feel a beautiful and positive emanation from him. I asked, 'Who are you?' He said 'I am the child of time.'

Then the room began to fill with people and a woman who seemed to be in charge. I wanted to give the baby the $100 bill but it was too crowded. The Child of Time was now up and looked like he might be five years old. He went upstairs to a booth. Soon there were multiple projections of movies and images on the walls. Then I found myself outside the building. It was made of bricks and was not square but staggered layers of different sized floors. Soon there were openings and a small space craft appeared and zoomed off, disappearing instantly. I thought this was a very significant way to begin the Year of the Dragon with The Child of Time!"

Disembodied Voices

The concept of receiving instruction in dreams is a time honored one. These messages can come from the voices of people we know or have known or from totally unrecognizable voices. Many have reported hearing voices that seem to come from "Teachers" imparting important information. Others mention teachings that come toward morning, and note that they feel as if they are overhearing words that are being impersonally transmitted. I have also heard dreamers speak of simply knowing they received information in their dreams *without* having heard it and without being able to remember just what it is. Yet, rather than being frustrated by this, they report an uncanny sense of satisfaction even without consciously knowing what the information is.

Life Dreams

Some dreams seem to reveal the structure of our lives and open up new vistas or edges for our open viewing. They usually have a momentous feeling to them and can be used by the dreamer as a big assist to self understanding. One of mine occurred during a difficult time in my life when I was writing and researching my memoir, *Pride of Family; Four Generations of American Women of Color*. The book was inspired by my great grandmother's 1868 diary and it documents my search for self understanding through my family heritage The dream is as vivid and important to me today as the time I dreamed it some 15 years ago:

"I am standing in front of a big old house, a kind of a mansion. It is a museum really, and tour groups are going in to visit it. I go in with them and I am moving through the large and elegant, but deserted rooms, when I realize that many of the others have gone ahead. Suddenly a little girl appears from behind a wall. She beckons to me and indicates I am not to let others know I have seen her. I know that she is a very determined little girl who is hiding in this house. She has been living here a long, long time. She only comes out when the visitors have left. I feel that she has been waiting years for this moment when she can talk to me. She takes my hand and leads me to the large glass window. I look out upon the beautiful but untended gardens out back. Fervently she whispers to me, "All of this is ours. You and I can get this house back if we want to."

Mandalas

Geometric patterns that appear in dreams can signal a highly meditative state in the dreamer, or the potential for same. I recommend painting or drawing them in waking state. In addition to the value of exploring the dream of reality and the reality of the dream in this manner, the resulting work may be used as a means of reentering dream state or as a powerful contemplative tool.

Recurrent Dreams

We work through our dream themes much as a painter will work through a phase in her art work. For example, "Father Dreams" may continue to pop up until we come to terms with that relationship. An entire story will frequently repeat in our dreams until we have moved through the stuck place in our psyches. Many of the recurring dreams I hear have fairly uncomfortable or unpleasant content. Here's one that also contains a fairly common kind of anxiety dream set-up-a kind of generic "On Stage Dream":

"I am thrust onstage: I do not know the lines or the dance steps. I am puzzled and terrified. Everyone else knows what they're doing but me. I try to pretend I know them. I feel horribly humiliated. I awaken feeling ashamed and devastated."

This dreamer continued to have variations on this dream for about a year, until finally, after some changes had occurred in her life, she was thrust onstage in a dream, and though at first she thought she did not know her lines, she found that they came to her, and spoke them softly. After some additional time had passed, she had a dream in which she was speaking onstage rather loudly to an approving audience.

Another recurrent dream told to me when I was recently lecturing in West Virginia dovetails with the classic "Falling Dream":

Each time I dream this dream, I am pushed off of a cliff. I fall and fall and wake up as I'm hitting the ground.

I was unable to follow this dreamer's progress, but, in addition to suggesting she work with a good counselor, I gave her the following techniques:

Either telling the dream aloud or writing the dream down and completing the dream in the most harmonious way possible can mark the beginning of a successful way of moving through. (This dreamer might do best to begin at the point where she is being pushed by the aggressor, taking a stance in her writing that would transform the moment in the most powerful way she can think of. The idea must come from herself, not from another.) This technique can also be surprisingly effective with pesky nightmares or other troubling moments in dreams. Remember, the psyche is listening, and the psyche is *you*. If you can imagine good or powerful actions on your part, you also have the potential of creating them in waking state. Your dreams can change in response to changes in your way of thinking and your way of being; and your life can change in response to dream changes. Breakthrough can occur in either direction!

(Based on our earlier commentary on the Senoi Community of Dreamers; if the above dreamer belonged to such a community, her family might try to give her the following tools:

1. Recognize that you're dreaming

2. Call upon a dream helper to combat the adversary

3. Turn around to face the adversary—then become more powerful than the adversary

4. Transform that adversary into something harmless, like a butterfly.

5. Get a gift from the adversary

Totems

> *"In the beginning of all things, wisdom and knowledge were with the animals' for Tirawa, the One Above, did not speak directly to man. He sent certain animals to tell men that he showed himself through the beasts, and that from them, and from the stars and the sun and the moon, man should learn" Chief Letakots-Lesa of the Pawnee tribe to Natalie Curtis, c. 1904*

The appearance of an animal, such as a leopard or a crow or a squirrel can also indicate that the qualities of that totem are useful to and available on an inner level to the dreamer. Totems can also be considered messengers from the other world or guides to deeper experiences. In many indigenous systems of dreaming, animals are revered for the messages they bring. My own primary dream totems are spotted cats, ranging from the playful ocelot that got the whole thing started for me some years back, to the powerful snow lion that recently strolled casually past me.

Joseph Campbell writes of early New York State Native American practices: "Not only was the clan totem reverenced, but each individual had his personal totem (in Algonquin manitou, in Iroquois aki) In youth after certain exercises and fastings he waited for a dream and whatever he had dreamed of became his manitou on which his fortune depended."

Composer and Master Mask Maker Norman Lowery had two inter-connecting dreams at Rose Mountain:

"I'm in a large meadow. There are wild strawberries everywhere and I am enjoying eating them immensely.

A large crow flies low overhead and I decide to follow. She leads me through some woods to the entrance to a cave."

Into the cave—it's not clear most of the time—palatial at times, glowing, jewel-like. I first see a green light. Before long I realize that what I will find in this cave is my mother. This makes me cry—also with some fear, thinking 'Oh no—this isn't what I want!' The cave is sometimes full of stalactites and stalagmites. I have to put on various ceremonial robes. Within all the swirling is the realization that I am reliving my life backwards-to infancy, to birth-the cave is a womb. I am reborn."

My friend and colleague, Andrea Goodman had a powerful totem dream a few days before we left for an Egyptian Mysteries Retreat at Nechung Dorje Drayang Ling Monastery in Hawaii.

"Owl Dream:

I am with Ione and a group of women, walking through the woods. We are moving through the trees, not on the ground but up among the branches. I am in a tree and look up and see the Great Snowy Owl. It is right above me. I realize it is about to poop and just in time I move back just enough so as not to be in the line of fire. I am that in tune with it. The owl suddenly opens its great wings and lifts off. Everyone gasps, it is so magnificent. It lifts up and then lands on my shoulders, one claw on each shoulder. It squeezes me too hard and I say, 'Beautiful Owl, please don't squeeze me so tight!'

A few months later, in Hawaii, we were on our way from a restaurant to the retreat center to my ordination ceremony, with Ione and a group of women. I was driving the van. As we turned onto the road leading to the retreat center, an owl flew right in front of us, leading the way ahead of us through the trees."

Puns

Dreams love to pun. Dreams like to play with the sounds of words. It's up to you to call them on it, and catch on. Sometimes it's a visual as well as verbal pun. In one of my earliest Dream Workshops in Saratoga Springs we all kept trying to understand Betsy's rabbit dream. Finally I asked her to describe the creature. It turned out that it had very long ears. "That's no rabbit," I exclaimed, "That's a hare!"

At that moment Betsey realized that the dreams were about the ongoing feud she'd been having with her father about her super long "hair".

Time Coding

Be on the alert for what I call "Time Codes". For example, you may find yourself in a regular modern day dream, only to notice a 1970s car parked at a corner of the street. This car may be a clue that at least part of your dream is connected to events that occurred in your waking life during that time period.

Aura of the Dream

What I call the"aura" might also be called the tone of a dream. (This is not always the emotional tone, but often just a subtle sense of the dream without content.) Even if there is no recall of imagery, just honoring the *quality* of the "aura" can be helpful. Sometimes a faint image will emerge as one basks in the aura of a dream. This could take the form of a color, a shape, or even the smallest fragment of an object. From these small clues, one could allow entire scenarios to unfold.

Universal Dream Themes

Some dreams resonate with our most personal problems while also speaking to the most universal of themes. Author Patricia Garfield has recently identified "The Universal Dream", classifying unifying dream themes that transcend cultures. She writes in a preliminary description of her forthcoming book on the subject "We've all had them—those alarming dreams of being chased by something grisly, a loved one getting hurt or dying, driving a car without brakes, not knowing the answers to a test, falling fearfully through the air, appearing naked or half-dressed in public, or racing for the train that has just departed. These and other bad dreams that everyone experiences at some point in their lives are too familiar. What most of us don't realize is that these very same dreams are universal. They have existed from before the beginning of recorded literature, and will occur tonight in every country of our planet. They cross different cultures and classes. They endure over time."

Archetypal Beings, Landscapes and Elements:

Wise Old Men and Wise Old Women are universal archetypes identified in our time by Jung. These elders—sometimes frightening, sometimes kindly and benevolent, appear in our dreams to give us teachings, inspirations, and sometimes scoldings.

Before taking a group to Egypt recently, I asked participants to send me a dream that was important in their lives. Here is the dream that graphic designer/photographer Robert Graf e-mailed me:

"Before leaving Minneapolis for New York City, I dreamed that I came to a mountain.

There was a tunnel at the base and a bearded old white haired man was standing there in weathered old clothing. I asked him if this was the correct tunnel. He said yes. I asked him how wide and high and how long. He said three feet by three feet and 900 miles long. I entered the dark tunnel without a light. That was the end of it."

It is interesting to note that the number nine is the number of another white haired archetype, the traditional figure of The Hermit in the Tarot—a figure who traditionally carries a lighted lamp of wisdom into the darkness.

Mountains, tunnels and caves all resonate deeply with the human psyche. Subways are a fun modern day addition to the timeless imagery of caves and tunnels; they are evocative locations of the underworld and other hidden recesses of our psyches.

The powerful element of water relates to intuition and feelings, and we can usually tell just where we are emotionally by the condition of the water in our dreams. Is the water in your dreams dirty, pristine and calm? Do you dream of powerful waves? All can indicate the state of your feelings. For example two friends who were both in strained marriages, told me, their dreams of water within days of each other. In one dream, the water was raging down the walls of the house. In the other, murky water was undermining the pillars and floor beams of her home.

Dreams of ice and snow, I've noticed can also be indicators of frozen or cold feelings. The bridges in our dreams can also be telling. How do we get from one place to another in our lives, from one job to another, or one relationship to another? How do we maneuver other kinds of changes?. The condition of the bridges and the very material of which they are built will tell us, as well as the way in which we cross them or hang off of them. Better check out the terrain or water they're crossing over as well, for more resonance with the vicissitudes of the waking state.

The following dream fragments by my painter and sculptor friend, Raquel Rabinovich, who was moving through creative challenges at the time she dreamed them, show how landscape and weather in our dreams can mirror our inner processes. While commenting on the present, such dreams can also comment on the qualities of an entire life's journey. Certainly, they also show qualities of concentration and determination to reach her destination, so if she were to apply the question, "How active or passive am I in these dreams?" There would be no doubt about the answer.

The Mountain: I was walking on a flat land. Suddenly, the earth caved in, creating almost insurmountable steep precipices and elevations which I had to traverse if I wanted to survive and eventually get to my destination. There was wind, ice, snow. All was in a constant state of flux, slippery, difficult. I was scared and feared not to have enough physical energy. I didn't stop, though I did stumble a few times. I continued my extremely difficult journey. Finally, I got to my destination and woke up.

The Oceans: I was driving on a wide two way road and on both sides the sea was intensely blue and extended to the infinite. As I was driving I would always see three straight lines. The one in the middle of the road, the one on my left at the edge of the sea, and the one on my right, also at the edge of the sea. Gradually all began to blur and to darken until all the lines disappeared. Though I knew my references were gone, that I could crash with another car coming from the other side of the road, or that I could fall into the sea, I did continue driving. The speed remained steady. I felt challenged, confident, excited, unaffected by any uncertainty or danger. I got to my destination and woke up.

Brook Dailey was a student of Pauline Oliveros in Atlanta when, in response to a class assignment., she reported a dream whose meaning is still unfolding for her. The dream contains very specific sensations, sounds, and colors and a beautiful, distorted landscape. You might notice how the dream makes you feel. What is happening in your own mind and body—what feelings come over your as you read Brook's Dream:

"When I was sixteen, I dreamt I had glass hands. They were quite precious and strange, with a gentle pink tint and a smooth, sleek finish. You could see right through them. My glass hands were unusually light-weight and were attached to my wrists with blue velvet ribbons. Throughout most of the dream, I sat peacefully, silently under a huge oak tree at sunset, a full blue moon rising. I stared curiously at my glistening, pink-tinted palms. The air was thick and I was thirsty. It began to rain. Large, fat, full drops fell from heavy clouds and tumbled clumsily to the earth. The only sound was that of the raindrops as they seemed to bounce off the grass and leaves. I placed my delicate glass hands over my eyes and watched the rain fall and the sun set and the moon rise. The view was colorful, distorted and beautiful.

I woke up from this dream and remembered it so vividly I thought I was still sitting under the oak, my hands made of glass. It was the most indescribably amazing feeling and the images of the dream were a truly awesome sight. I have since tried to capture the beauty of the dream through drawings and watercolor paintings, but I never seem to get it right, especially the colors."

A Few Deep Dreaming ™Exercises

COLOR DREAMING

Notice the function of color in your dreams. Try tracking your dream palette to discover what different colors mean to you. I have noticed that many dreamers arrive at my home or office unconsciously wearing the colors and outfits that match the feelings and attitudes that are prominent in their dreams. In a stunning and funny break through from dream to waking state, a lovely blonde patient who had been just that morning startled to hear herself called a "little gorilla" by a lover, came to see me. She was completely unconscious of the synchronicity of the black fuzzy sweater she had donned in the morning. I wasn't surprised to hear that she had dreamed of monkeys.

EARLY CHILDHOOD DREAMING

Recall your earliest dream, or an important childhood dream. Ask yourself how this dream may still have meaning for you as an adult. Arnold Mindell suggests that our early childhood dreams often have a relationship to our adult body symptoms.

FAMILY DREAMING

Record the dreams of your life partner and/or other members of your family. You may be surprised to find that you are sharing similar dream images on any given night! As I mentioned earlier, I discovered this on my own in the early 1970s and was interested to find that Dr. Edward Bynum has recently described the phenomenon in his book, *Families and the Interpretation of Dreams: Awakening the Intimate Web.*

FLYING DREAMS

Try inventing a new flying method. Enjoy flying in your dream. Take yourself to a special place. Notice how others respond to your flying. Their responses often indicate how you feel others relate to your personal abilities. What is special about your flying method? In my collection of flying methods there are some quite inventive ones. Some flap their arms like wings, others enjoy the straight armed superman style, still others go for push ups, leaps and pogo stick type hops. Gliding, floating and swimming, and skating, when they are effortless and full of good feeling are, to my way of thinking, all a part of the *flying* syndrome. Here is poet Chie Hasegawa's flying dream from her book in collaboration with George Quasha: *Ainu Dreams:*.

> *This flying says it for me.*
> *I mean I want to be known*
> *by what it shows,*
> *How I angle my wings,*
> *The lift of the feather*

Against the air, the look
That blows across my face,
Body turning out
Of itself, tellingly.
If you want to know me,
Just keep watching
For a space of time.

EATING IN DREAMS

Notice the function of food in your dreams. Can you taste food? How often do you dream of restaurants and other places that might symbolize nourishment? My Dream Groups would periodically have dream get-togethers and bring food and drink that they had dreamed. This created quite interesting fare, as you can imagine, ranging from a peculiar lop-sided cake to the spare ribs dreamed up by a struggling vegetarian.

LEXICON OF DREAMS

Create a lexicon of your own personal dream symbols and their meanings as they unfold over the course of time. You may find some unusual meanings that are yours alone that belong to no pre-existing theories. For example, Laura Donnelly discovered that cars in her dreams equated with her soul.

DREAM MAPS AND DIAGRAMS

The *location* of the events in our dreams is very important. Diagrams and maps assist us in becoming acquainted with the territory of our psyches. For example, in a dream of one's childhood home, noticing where events take place can give additional information about the message from the dream. Does the action take place in the kitchen? In your old bedroom? In your parents' room? Sometimes large areas of terrain are covered in dreams, and mapping them out can be both fun and instructive. If you would like to be more elaborate, create collages or paintings of the most important areas. Go further, try keeping a completely word-less journal for a while.

DREAM MEDITATION

Lying on one side, begin to follow your breathing. Focus on the out breath. Gradually allow yourself to slip into sleep meditating. Swami Sivananda Radha, author of *Realities of the Dreaming Mind* suggests that you sleep on your left side and breathe through the left nostril by keeping the right one closed. Remain mindful of your intention as you have been in waking state. She strongly recommends you bring to mind a mantra and visualize and think about the Divine Light as you fall asleep. "Maintain focus on the divine and surrender to the wisdom within." There are many other methods of meditating in dreams, and varying opinions among spiritual teachers as to which side one should sleep on. You could research the one that is best for you, using the bibliography in this handbook.

DREAM MEMORIES

Notice the function of memory in your dreams. Do you "remember" things while dreaming that only pertain to the dream world? How often have you visited a place that you remember in a dream.

only to realize upon waking that it has no waking significance to you? Or has the opposite occurred? You find a place in waking state that you know you've visited before. (Was it in a dream?) Does the phenomenon of Déjà vu pertain to dreams? Do you sometimes remember important information while dreaming? Find lost objects? How well can you remember your waking suggestions about dreaming while you are still asleep? Try developing new ways of remembering these suggestions.

DREAM MOVEMENT

Create a full out dance of a special dream. Or just do a simple, short dream dance for yourself one morning. Notice how you move in dreams. What kind of gestures do you and your dream characters make in your dreams.? Sharing dreams using gesture alone (no words or sounds) can be very powerful and often reveals more about the dream than words could ever accomplish.

DREAM LISTENING

Begin to pay attention to the function of listening in your dreams. What kinds of sounds occur while you're dreaming? Do you integrate alarms and outside voices into your dream content?

Go into sleep humming or making soft sounds. Who composes the music you hear in your dreams? Make sounds (not words) that express the feelings, characters, objects and landscapes of your dreams.

Try dreaming a song or chant that has special meaning for you.

What languages do you speak or understand in dreams? A French actress I met recently spoke of dreams in which she can speak special non-existent (in waking state) languages, **which are completely understood by her dream characters.**

DREAM SHARING

Have you ever found out that you and a close friend had shared all or part of the same dream? This phenomenon is an old one, annotated in many ancient Indian texts. I have observed it most often between lovers or spiritual partners (the two are not mutually exclusive) who are intensely communing with each other. Sun Bear, in *Dreaming with the Medicine Wheel*, offers a Meditation to Dream Together. Members of Dream Circles soon find that their dreams begin to interweave themes and symbols. We have incubated dreams of going to certain locations together, like Paris, or a fabulous beaches with some success. Members of my Mysteries Circles practice dreaming together with regularity.

A DREAM JOURNAL PROCESS

This process has been adapted from a system I learned some years ago from a dedicated dream worker. It is a comparatively linear way of tracing your dreams in an ongoing journal. If you don't have time to write out your entire dream; try taking notes in the morning, or at night if you awaken, with a handy night light pen and dream journal, or use any old pen and a simple pad of paper. Then when you have a quiet moment, write the whole dream out. Important. Don't worry if you don't remember your dreams every single morning. Since dreams dislike rigidity, just honor them and enjoy them when they do arise. When writing in your dream journal, you can try to remain in dream state as long as possible. Give your waking, over judgmental self a rest. Whatever comes is fine.

Marisol's Dream: "In my dream a crazy clown breaks into my house and steals my bracelet. I am really scared, but then a policeman who happened to be passing by comes in the front door. I try to tell him what is going on, but he just stands there looking at the clown who starts casually lounging on the sofa. He won't do anything to help me. The clown jumps out the window and then peers back inside, kind of leering at me with the bracelet draped over its nose. I awaken very upset and can't get the feeling to go away during the day."

1. Title: Title your dream.

2. Feeling: What are the feelings in the dream.? Usually there is one primary feeling. Or you may have a feeling that shifts, say from anger to joy, or vice-versa. Just jot that down.

3. Theme: What is the theme of your dream? Any ongoing themes? Perhaps this is a "mother' dream, or perhaps it is a "back to school" dream.

4. First Question: Ask the dream a question. There will usually be one very evident question that comes to mind. But you can also get very interesting results from asking questions of different characters or even objects in your dream. You can try putting yourself back in the dream in your imagination and asking away. Jot down whatever comes.

5. Second Question: Ask: "What question is this dream asking me?"

6. Third Question: Ask: "How active or passive am I in this dream? Do things just happen to me in this dream or do I make things happen?".

7. Extrapolate and substitute: In order to open up the dream more fully, you may want to trim away details or descriptions that hide more basic dream meanings from you.

8. Associate: Let your mind drift a bit. Notice any puns, associations, ideas, images, or memories that occur to you when you bring the dream to mind. Follow the threads until you get one or more "hits".

9. Play: Play with the dream by using any of the exercises in this handbook. Create your own ways of playing with and exploring your dream and the elements of your dream.

Marisol's Dream Journal Work:

Title your Dream: Marisol titled her dream *Break in*

Feeling: She noted that the primary emotion was *fear*. Her upset at the end felt like a mixture of fear and frustration, maybe with some anger mixed in. She wrote this down too.

Theme: She had had other dreams in which items had been stolen from her, so she wrote down *Theft* as the theme. She'd also had other dreams about her bracelet ; which was one that had been given to her by a former boyfriend. So she added, *bracelet dream*, thereby giving the dream two themes. Marisol then tried to put herself back into the dream world, imagining herself in the same room again facing the policeman.

First Question: What question do I have for this dream?
Marisol decided to ask a part of the dream a question. Though she could have chosen any part at all, including both animate and inanimate aspects of the dream, she chose the Dream Policeman:
"Why didn't you protect me and arrest that thieving clown?"

In Marisol's imagination the Dream Policeman replied, *"You were never in any real danger and besides, I really have a healthy respect for humor."*

Marisol realized that the dream was commenting on her tendency to face life in an overly serious manner. She could still feel the fear in the dream and related it to her waking fear of letting down her aloofness with others. (This was, in fact a large factor in her break up with the former boyfriend who'd given her the bracelet.) She remembered that she actually admired funny women and secretly harbored a fantasy of wanting to be a comedian or a comedy writer herself. The memory came back to her that as a child she had been enamored of the clowns in the circus! Why was she so fearful then about this clown? She also thought about how she'd always been interested in the way certain birds were attracted to shiny objects, prankishly stealing them for their nests.

Second Question: What Question is the Dream Asking Me?
In asking what question the dream was asking her, Marisol reimagined (redreamed) the clown and saw her wearing the bracelet on her glowing nose. It was a "light-bulb moment". She got the idea. The question from the dream was: "Why don't you Lighten up?" Not only did this seem a general comment on her life, but she thought it signaled that it was time for her to let loose of her obsessive thoughts about her old boyfriend.

Third Question: How Active or Passive am I in this dream?: Marisol saw that although the most familiar part of herself, the part that was fearful, and had felt fairly helpless in the dream, the clown figure or aspect of herself was quite forthright and daring. The Dream Police (She thought of him as her self policing mechanism, but also connected him with her father's disapproving ways.) had actively refused to arrest or stop the funny part of her from emerging. She sensed from this that she was beginning to let down her guard.

Extrapolate and Substitute: Instead of thinking "clown"—Marisol tried substituting "a carefree, funny man", instead of Policeman, she imagined "authority figure", and so on.

Play: Marisol decided to play with this dream by getting tickets for the circus which was coming to town very soon. She got some hair coloring and gave herself a magenta streak and she also got herself a quirky new bracelet these things and others she was beginning to imagine, made her feel rather daring and good. She put the old bracelet away in a drawer.

Conclusion

Dreams are available to all of us. Dreams are not only free, but they represent the most palpable proof that we ourselves are free. They help us to unfold the stories and feelings that are important to our well being in the world. We find when we share dreams with friends, family, lovers, even without knowing at the outset what they "mean", that the intimacy we long for is suddenly available to us. We have but to pay attention to our dreams, to listen deeply to what they have to tell us, to reveal ourselves to ourselves. By becoming Deep Dreamers we are put in contact with what Chogyam Trungpa Rinpoche calls our own basic goodness. When we explore the "Dream of Reality and the Reality of the Dream" we begin to experience ourselves as an integral part of the dreaming universe.

END

Abram,David, *The Spell of the Sensuous,* Vintage Books, 1996

Aristotle, *On Dreams, J.I. Beare, Translator*

Bachelor. Stephen, *Verses from the Center; A Buddhist Vision of the Sublime,* Riverhead, April 2000

Bluestone, Sarvananda, *The World Dream Book,* Destiny Books, Rochester, Vermont, 2002

Bosnak, Robert, *A Little Course in Dreams*—Shambhala Press Bosnak, Robert, Dreaming With an Aids Patient, Shambhala Press, 1989

Bovoso, Antonio, Leigh Rollin, *Cats in Black Shoes,* 1985

Bovoso, Alessandro & Ione, Sandro's Dreams (Manuscript)

Brook, Stephen, The Oxford Book of Dreams, Oxford University Press, 1987

Bynum, Edward, Families and the Interpretation of Dreams: Awakening the Intimate Web.

(Harrington Park Press)

Burnside and Robotham, *Spirits of the Passage, The Transatlantic Slave Trade in the Seventeenth Century,* Simon and Schuster, 1997

Campbell, Joseph, The Hero with a Thousand Faces Bollingen Series/Princeton 1973

Campbell, Joseph, *Historical Atlas of World Mythology Vol.1: The Way of the Animal Powers*

Part 2:Mythologies of the Great Hunt Volume 2 Part 2 The Way of the Seeded Earth, Harper and Row

Cayce, Edgar, (Many Titles) ARE Press

The Dalai Lama, *Sleeping, Dreaming, and Dying*—Wisdom Books, 1997

Epel, Naomi, *Writers Dreaming*—Vintage Books, 1993

Garfield, Patricia, Ph.D. *The Dream Messenger*—Simon and Schuster,1997

Garfield, Patricia, Ph.D. *Creative Dreaming*—Fireside Press, 1995

Garfield, Patricia, Ph.D. *Pathway to Ecstasy*—Prentice Hall Press, 1979

Garfield, Patricia,Ph.D. *Women's Bodies, Women's Dreams* Ballantine Books, 1988

Garrard, Ana Lora, An Invitation to Dream; Tap the Resources of Inner Wisdom, Llewellyn Publications, 1993

Guiley, Rosemary Ellen, *Dreamwork for the Soul; A Spiritual Guide to Dream Interpretation,* The Berkeley Publishing Group

Hart, Corriere, Karle, Woldenberg, *Dreaming and Waking*—The Center Foundation Press, Inc.

Harary, Ph.D., and Pamela Weintraub, Lucid Dreams in 30 Days; The Creative Sleep Program, St. Martin's Press, New York,1989

Hayman, R.I.P., *Dreamsound Pillow Notes*, 1986

Hayman, R.I.P. *Listening to Dreams* ; A Project for Middle Ear Muscle Activity Audio Level Telemetry-Article: *Current Research in Arts Medicine* Med Arts International; a cappella books, 1993

Hillman, James *The Dream and the Underworld*—Harper and Row,1975

Ione, Carole, *Pride of Family; Four Generations of American Women of Color*, Avon Books, 1993

Jouvet, Michel, The Paradox of Sleep; The story of Dreaming

Jung,C.G, *Memories, Dreams, Reflections*, Vintage Books, 1965

Kaplan-Williams, Strephon, Dream Cards, Fireside, Simon & Schuster 1991

Krippner, Stanley, *Dreamtime & Dreamwork-; Decoding The Language of the Night*—Tarcher, St. Martin's Press, 1990

Larsen, Stephen,Ph.D. *The Mythic Imagination*, Bantam Paperback, 1990

La Berge, Stephen, Ph.D.*Lucid Dreaming*—Ballantine Books, 1985

Martin, Stephan A., *Smaller Than Small, Bigger Than Big,The Role of the "Little Dream" in Individuation.*, Quadrant XXV, vol 2 (1992)

Mellick, Jill, *The Natural Artistry of Dreams*—Conari Press,1996

Merchant, Carolyn, *The Death of Nature*—Harper and Row, 1980

Mindell, Arnold *Dreaming While Awake: Techniques for 24 Hour Lucid Dreaming,* Hampton Roads Publishing Company.2000

Mindell, Arnold, *Quantum Mind; The Edge Between Physics and Psychology* Lao Tse Press,2000

Mindell, Arnold *Working with the Dreaming Body*—Arkana Press,1989

Mindell, Arnold, *The Shaman's Body*, Harper Collins, 1993 (Also many other recommended titles)

Norbu, Namkhai, Dream Yoga and the Practice of Natural Light, Snow Lion Publications,1992

Oliveros, Pauline, DM, *Deep Listening: A Composer's Sound Practice*, forthcoming from Deep Listening Publications in 2005

Pritchard, Evan T., *No Word for Time* ; *The Way of the Algonquin People*, Council Oaks Books,1997

Quasha, George, Hasegawa, Chie (buun) *Ainu Dreams*, Station Hill Press, 1999

Ratcliffe, Stephen, *Listening to Reading*, SUNY Press, NY.

Reed, Henry, *Getting Help from Your Dreams*, Ballantine Books, 1988

Reed, Henry, *Dream Solutions, Dream Realizations: Discover Intuitive Guidance in your Dreams,*Hermes Home Press, 1996

Shafton, Anthony, *Dream Singer;The African American Way With Dream.*

John Wiley and Sons, Inc. 2002

Shlain, Leonard, *The Goddess Versus The Alphabet ; The Conflict Between Word and Image*—Penguin Arkana, 1999

Sivananda Radha, Swami—*Realities of the Dreaming Mind,* Timeless Books

Stewart, RJ., *Dream Power Tarot*—Thorsons/Harper Collins, San Francisco 1993

Sun Bear, *Dreaming with the Medicine Wheel*—Fireside Press,1994

Surya Das, Lama, *Tibetan Dream Yoga,* Sounds True Audio Cassettes

Trungpa, Chogyam, Shambhala; *The Sacred Path of the Warrior*—Shambhala Press, 1978

Van De Castle, Robert L.,*Our Dreaming Mind*—Ballantine Books, 1994

Ullman, M, Krippner, S. and Vaughan, A, *Dream Telepathy: Experiments in Nocturnal ESP,* MacFarland, 1989

Wangyal, Tenzin Rinpoche,*The Tibetan Yogas of Dream and Sleep*—Snow Lion Publications
Journals,1998

Wolf, Fred Alan Ph.D *The Dreaming Universe,* Simon and Schuster, 1994

Zimmer, Tim—*Sound in Dreams* (Manuscript, A Paper For Pauline Oliveros' Deep Listening Class at RPI), 12/06/02

Dream Network: A Journal Exploring Dreams and Myth The New Millennium; A Journal For Times of Change and Transformation: Dimensions of Dreaming, A.R.E. Press, October/November 1999 Issue Ions—Noetic Sciences Review, All Issues 1998,99 and Jan–June 2000

http://www.ASDreams.com
www.dreamgate.com/electric-dreams
Dream @intuition.org
www.intuitions.org
www.onelist.com/subscribe.cgi/MorpheusDreams

THIS BOOK IS A PROJECT OF DEEP LISTENING PUBLI-
CATIONS
PO BOX 1956
KINGSTON, NY, 12401

Please see The Deep Listening Catalog and Deep Listening Label
for the work of the following composers and many others:
<www.deeplistening.org>

Joe Catalano

Andrea Goodman

R.I.P. Hayman

Norman Lowery

Pauline Oliveros

Scott Smallwood

The Dream Sack: <www.deeplistening.org/ione/dreamsack.html>

IONE may be reached at <iodreams@deeplistening.org>
www.deeplistening.org/ione

Ione is dream facilitator, author, and educator who has taught
and lectured extensively throughout the United States and Europe.
Since the 1970s she has created small and large Dream Events and
Festivals in many cities. Most recently she has been creating *Ione's
Dream Festival* annually in the New York's Hudson Valley. Ione is
also a psychotherapist specializing in the creative process, heritage,
myths and dreams. She is the Founding Minister of the Ministry of
Maat, Inc., and regularly recreates ancient rituals at the sacred sites
of Egypt. She is the author of the acclaimed memoir, ***Pride of Family, Four Generations of American Women of Color;*** Doubleday/

Broadway Books,2004. She is Playwright and Director of the international work, ***Njinga, The Queen King; The Return of a Warrior,*** with Sound Design and Original Music by Pauline Oliveros and the Dance Opera ***Io and Her and the Trouble with Him.***

0-595-33448-2

Printed in the United States
By Bookmasters